Creative
textile art

~ to be re.

Creative
textile art
Techniques and projects

Karen Woods

A & C Black · London

First published in Great Britain in 2010
A & C Black Publishers Limited
36 Soho Square
London W1D 3QY
www.acblack.com

ISBN 978-1-4081-2339-3

Copyright © Karen Woods 2010

CIP Catalogue records for this book are available from
the British Library and the US Library of Congress.

Karen Woods has asserted her right under the
Copyright, Design and Patents Act 1988 to be identified
as the author of this work.

Typeset in 10 on 14pt Celeste
Book design by Susan McIntyre
Cover design by Saffron Stocker
Publisher: Susan James

Printed in China by C&C Offset Printing Co., Ltd.

This book is produced using paper that is made from
wood grown in managed, sustainable forests. It is
natural, renewable and recyclable. The logging and
manufacturing processes conform to the environmental
regulations of the country of origin.

Contents

ACKNOWLEDGEMENTS

Thanks to everyone who helped make this book happen: Nic Barfield, for his support and patience; Chris Webb for all the workshop photography, often done at short notice; Gina Marsh and Livvy Penrose for modelling the jewellery pieces; and artists Samantha Bryan and Sue Macdonald for allowing me to show images of their work in the *Heads* project, page 76.

FOREWORD

Textile art is an imaginative and versatile craft which can be used to recreate flat, 2-D work, and, when combined with other media, can bring 3-D objects to life. This book aims to show how textiles need not be restricted to surface decoration. The multitude of materials, techniques and patterns can be harnessed by the textile artist in a structured yet creative way, in much the same way as an illustrator, sculptor or other visual artist does.

Creativity is also encouraged at every stage in the book, as it is a vital element of artistry; each project offers a finished piece if you follow its instructions step-by-step, but experimentation and adaption will allow you to branch out into your own projects while you learn the skills and techniques explained. This can often be done with recycled materials, which feature prominently in the projects. Using these can be immensely rewarding, as you end up with a unique final piece which gives new life to old objects. It also helps to keep your materials budget to a minimum!

In short, don't worry about how polished your technique is or how expensive your tools and materials are: just learn to look at things with new eyes and engage with everything around you. Creativity is an ongoing process, and textiles and mixed media allow artists the perfect medium for building their personal and cultural identities into their works. This book will help you to do the same.

1 Brooch

This brooch (or corsage, to give it a posh name) is created using leather off-cuts and fabric scraps which are layered and given depth and texture with cutwork and bead decoration. We also used a specialist heat iron (a pyrographic tool) for 'burning in' marks for the surface decoration, though this is optional – using a punch to mark the leather, or simply stitching into it, will both work equally well.

TECHNIQUES |||||||||||||||||||||||||||||||||

- Designing and drawing a brooch
- Cutting
- Fraying
- Free machine embroidery
- Appliqué
- Beading
- Marking materials with heat

MATERIALS ||||||||||||||||||||||||||||||||||||||

- Heat-fix web adhesive or Bondaweb
- Scrap fabrics
- Leather off-cuts
- Hand and machine threads
- Iron and ironing board
- Small beads, recycled jewellery
- Beading needles, hand sewing needles
- Pyrographic tool such as a Fabric-Master

▶ *Drawing flower template on to card*

Bold, regular shapes are easiest to work with to create the layers of the brooch. You can copy bold floral designs from fabric or wallpaper, construct geometric shapes such as stars or diamonds, or use your imagination to draw a shape.

This project uses just two layers of leather cut into contrasting shapes, but there's no reason why you can't use three, four or even more.

▶ *Cutting out card template*

◀ *Two cut-out card templates, one for each layer*

Once you've got the bottom layers of the brooch designed, think about how to build up some depth in the centre of the brooch.

As in the 'Dead Cosy' project (p.100–115), a flat strip of fabric can be manipulated into a 3-D flower. Here, we're using a strip of cut and shaped soft leather to create a similar 'petal' effect.

First design a single frilly-edged freehand 'petal' as a master shape. Make sure it's fairly regular at both ends so that it joins up when it's in a repeat pattern.

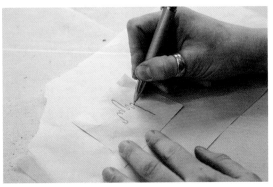

◀ *Drawing a master shape for a repeat pattern*

▶ *Copying the master pattern to create repeats*

Draw two parallel lines, with the distance between them the depth you want the 'petals' to be. Cut out your master 'petal', and then trace round it repeatedly along the strip.

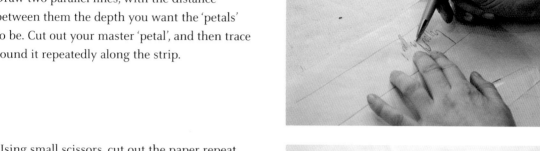

Using small scissors, cut out the paper repeat pattern to be used as a block template.

▶ *The cut-out repeat pattern template*

◀ *Tracing around the templates on to leather*

Transfer the template shapes for the base layers on to leather. We've used the same fairly thick leather for our two layers, but why not experiment with other weights of leather, contrasting colours, and other materials such as thin rubber, stiffened felt, backed fabrics and composites of several layers of material stuck together?

◀ *Cutting out the leather shapes*

11

▶ *Cutting through the leather*

Cutwork adds extra texture and depth.

A pyrographic tool such as a Fabric-Master comes with different tips which give different results when you burn into your chosen material. If you're using rubber or plastic, take extra care.

Top tip   Place the work on a board or kitchen block to prevent the pyrographic tool from burning into your table or worktop!

▶ *Marking the leather with a heat tool*

▶ *Transferring the repeat pattern on to fabric*

For the richly-fringed inner petals, we've chosen soft chamois-type leather. Make sure you pick a fairly thin leather or fabric.

Draw a baseline on the material, put the straight edge of the block template on it, and transfer your repeat. You'll need at least 30 cm of 'petal' strip, and it's probably best to make a bit extra.

Appliqué cut-outs can add extra interest to the design. Here we've used thin silver plastic (boiler insulation with the 'bubble' layer removed), and backed it with iron-on heat-fix web. We drew tiny teardrop shapes on the backing paper, and then cut them out.

▶ *Drawing small shapes on to back of heat-fix web*

▶ *Positioning cut-out appliqué details before fixing with iron*

Position the appliqué shapes carefully on the 'petal' strip, cover them with a piece of cloth, and iron them on to fix.

Put the work in an embroidery ring, drop the machine's teeth and fit a free machine embroidery foot. Then stitch round with small zig-zag or straight stitches.

▶ *Stitching round appliqué details*

◀ *Cutting out repeat-patterned strip*

Remove the work from the ring and carefully cut out the decorated strip.

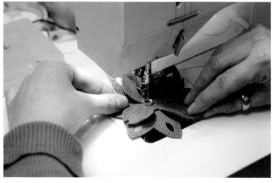

Use a strong needle or special leather needle to stitch the base layers together. You only need to stitch through the centre of your shapes – we stitched a small circle through both layers.

◀ *Stitching the leather base layers together*

▶ *Starting to create the 'petal'*

With the machine set to a small zig-zag stitch and the teeth dropped (as for free machine embroidery), hold one end of the leather strip and zig-zag over it to secure it to the backing leather.

As you zig-zag, slowly turn the leather strip around the needle so as to form a tightly stitched coil. With the frilly edge on the outside of the circle, work in a clockwise direction – moving the leather strip so that it touches the previously stitched strip.

When your 'flower' is getting near to your desired size, snip off the excess leather strip. Then finish sewing, and at the end, reverse backwards and then forwards to tie off the stitch securely.

▶ *Cutting leather strip to desired length*

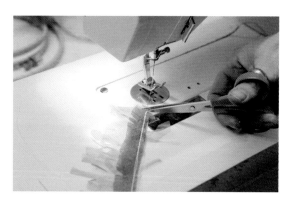

◀ *Layering several strips of lightweight fabric*

Cut equal-length strips of light fabrics such as organza, chiffon, tulle or net. Layer them, and then stitch a straight line along the bottom of the layered strip. It's best to put the machine's teeth up and put a normal sewing foot on, as this makes sewing a straight line considerably easier.

If you like, you can fray the top edges of the layered strips – just cut into them with small scissors, making sure you do not cut through the securing stitch along the baseline.

Using the same technique employed to create the leather centre petals, stitch the layered fabric strip tightly in a clockwise direction.

◀ *Stitching layered strip into petal centre*

Depending on how your 'flower' turns out, you might like to cut into the leather and fabric petals to produce an even frillier effect.

To create an interesting shiny highlight or to hide stitch lines, experiment with adding stitching cord, thin wire or pipe cleaners to your brooch. You'll need to set the machine to a small zig-zag stitch (but wide enough to sew over the wire or cord) and have a free machine embroidery foot fitted.

▶ *Sewing thin decorative wire over stitch lines*

▶ *Snipping away excess wire*

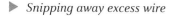

Use small electrical pliers or jewellers' pliers to snip off the excess wire or pipe cleaner.

If you'd like to add some decorative stamens, pierce a small hole through the centre of the flower using the point of your scissors or a bodkin.

▶ *Piercing through the centre of the flower*

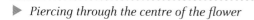

15

▶ *Adding glass stamens on florists' wire*

We bought some glass-ended florists' stamens, but you can easily make your own – see how we did this near the end of the 'Boil-Away Flowers' chapter, p.41–2.

Push the stamens through the hole and bend the ends back to secure them.

Putting a felt backing pad behind the bottom layer of the brooch will hold the decorative stamens in place and also provide a fixing point for the brooch clasp.

▶ *Putting a felt pad on the back of the brooch*

◀ *Trimming away excess felt*

When you stitch the pad in place, put it underneath the flower and stitch through from the top – close to the outside of the petals or along the decorative wire.

Finally, hand-stitch a bought brooch clasp or one salvaged from a piece of broken jewellery

If you want to adapt your brooch to make hair adornments or wrist corsages, substitute a big hairclip or some elastic ribbon for the brooch clasp. Alternatively, use a big old-fashioned hatpin to fix it to a hat.

◀ *Hand-stitching brooch clasp to backing*

▲ *Textile brooches also make eye-catching hair adornments*

2 Necklace

This project shows you how to create your own personalised, lavishly decorated necklace. You choose the imagery and materials to suit your look – ideas for the piece made in this chapter were gathered from decorative fabric samples, gardening books and wildlife books. You might like to look at historical costumes, comic-book characters or themes such as astrology, goth, punk – the choices are endless.

TECHNIQUES ||||||||||||||||||||||||||||||||||

- Designing and drawing a necklace
- Cutting
- Appliqué
- Free machine embroidery
- Beading
- Whipping

MATERIALS ||||||||||||||||||||||||||||||||||

- Water soluble fabric
- Heat-fixed web adhesive or Bondaweb
- Scrap fabrics
- Leather off-cuts
- Hand and machine threads
- Iron and ironing board
- Small beads, recycled jewellery
- Beading needles, hand sewing needles

Sketchbooks and pattern books can be great inspirations

Once you've picked your reference imagery, work out a shape that suits your neck. Slightly V-shaped designs like this one will sit comfortably on your collarbone.

▲ *Designing necklace template*

||||||||||||||||||||||||||||||||||||||||||||||||||||||||||||||||||||||||||||

Top tip   Experiment by cutting out shapes from different weights of fabric to see what hangs well and feels right.

||||||||||||||||||||||||||||||||||||||||||||||||||||||||||||||||||||||||||||

To make the base layer of the necklace, you'll need to layer interesting scraps of fabric on to the dissolvable fabric. Use heat-fix web adhesive on the back of the scraps, and then cut out the shapes you require. Build up your design using the cut-outs. Remember that the water-soluble fabric will 'boil away', so if you leave spaces in the overall necklace, these will eventually produce holes in the design – allowing either decorative backing fabric or your skin to show through.

If you have old fabrics with interesting patterns or detail such as fancy stitching, try cutting them up to create a rich background to the design.

▲ *Tracing image on to water-soluble fabric*

▲ *Cutting heat-fix web adhesive for backing*

▲ *Cutting stitched detail out of an old sari*

▷ *Ironing heat-fix web to back of fabric scrap*

If you wish to reproduce detailed images from your drawn design, it's best to trace fiddly shapes on to the paper backing of the heat-fix web, cut them out carefully and iron them on in the desired positions.

Build up your necklace by overlaying all your cut-outs on the design you drew on the water-soluble fabric.

Very carefully, cover the laid-on cut-outs with a cloth, then iron to fix.

▷ *Peeling away backing from heat-fix web*

▽ *Ironing on traced images for appliqué detail*

▲ *Laying on cut-out shapes before fixing with an iron*

◁ *Covering work with a cloth before ironing*

Top tip   For complex designs, it's a good idea to lay on and iron the cut-out shapes in stages.

21

When all the cut-outs have been fixed to the soluble fabric backing, place the work really tightly in an embroidery ring. Drop the teeth on your sewing machine, attach a darning foot or free machine embroidery foot, and set the stitch width to zero (for straight stitch).

For extra embellishment and texture, try loosening the tension on the bobbin case which contains the bottom thread. (Simply hold the bobbin case tightly in one hand and turn the screw on the side of the case for a couple of turns in an anti-clockwise motion to release the tension.) This has the effect of bringing the bottom thread to the surface of the design – you can use this to heighten the contrast between the top and bottom threads.

Here we've used a gold thread on the bottom and a pale yellow thread on the top.

Experiment with different types of threads in different tensions. Try tightening the top thread tension while the bottom tension remains loose – this brings the bottom colour even more to the fore. Remember to change the tension setting back once you've finished.

Keep changing the colours and build up the stitched designs until you're happy with the overall look.

▲ *Building up stitched detail with free machine embroidery*

▲ *Stitching extra colours into the design*

▲ *Trimming away excess water-soluble backing fabric*

Boil a pan of water to dissolve the backing fabric: it takes a couple of minutes for all the soluble fabric to disappear. Then, fish the work out with a pair of tongs or a wooden spoon.

Top tip   You can use a jug kettle to boil away the fabric if it's easier, but make sure to rinse it out well afterwards!

Carefully smooth the damp work with your fingers between two layers of absorbent fabric, and then iron it to dry and flatten it out.

Using a beading needle, stitch in beads, sequins, old bits of recycled jewellery, tiny electronic components – anything that's small, sparkly and doesn't weigh too much!

Putting a backing fabric behind the work will make the necklace more comfortable to wear. Here we've used soft chamois leather; felt also makes a good backing fabric because it doesn't fray and doesn't need edging.

▲ *Place the work carefully in a pan of boiling water*

▲ *Ironing the work to dry and flatten it out*

▲ *Adding beadwork decoration*

▲ *Stitching the work on to leather backing*

23

▶ *Trimming away excess leather*

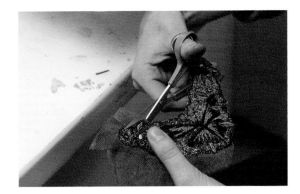

Your necklace will need a neck cord that's strong but light. Here we've used a thin coiled cord – fine upholstery cord, piping cord, ribbon or even thick hand-sewing thread will all do the job well.

Use a bodkin or the sharp end of a scissor blade to pierce a small, neat hole through which you can insert the cord. You can edge this hole to give extra strength and stop your decorative stitching from unravelling.

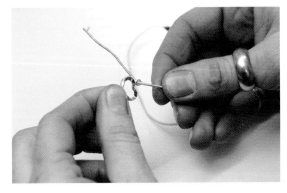

▶ *Threading end of cord to tie the necklace*

▶ *Whipping the cord to secure it*

Set your machine to a zig-zag stitch and, with a free embroidery foot fitted, secure the cord or ribbon by 'whipping' it. To do this, turn 2–3 cm of the cut end of the cord back on itself, and then stitch over both cords with the zig-zag stitch. Repeat the process to fix a second short length of cord to the other side of the necklace.

You might be happy to just tie the two lengths of neck cord or ribbon, but if you want a more professional finish, use a fastening. To do this, attach the two pieces of fastening to the ends of the neck cords using the 'whipping' technique shown in the previous step.

▶ *Attaching a fastening*

▶ *Decorating the whipping stitch with beads*

You may choose to decorate the neck cord, too. Small beads work well, or you could alternatively continue zig-zag stitching along the entire length of the cord.

▼ *Richly decorated textile necklaces make great evening wear*

3 Flowers

The flowers created in this project look great displayed in a vase or as single stems, and can be made using easily-sourced materials. The techniques are easy, too – simple hand stitching combined with machine work is all that's required. When you're confident, you can experiment with other materials to produce even bigger and bolder blooms.

TECHNIQUES ||||||||||||||||||||||||||||||||||||||

- Assembling a petal frame from wire
- Cutting
- Edging using satin stitch (machine stitch) and blanket stitch (hand sewing)
- Fabric manipulation
- Decorative French knots
- Wrapping tape

MATERIALS |||||||||||||||||||||||||||||||||||||

- Scrap fabrics
- Modelling wire or garden wire
- Hand and machine threads
- Thin gaffer tape or florists' tape
- Iron and ironing board

Create simple petal outline shapes by bending wire into evenly spaced loops, or 'fingers'. Five petals have been used in this flower.

▶ *Bending wire into petal shape*

▶ *Cutting the wire with wire cutters*

Leave the wire longer on the first and last petals – we've left about 12–15 cm. This allows the ends to be joined at the seam to form a complete flower. Next, position two ironed pieces of fabric as shown, placing the bottom piece face down and the top piece face up.

Set your sewing machine to a zig-zag stitch with the stitch width at the maximum setting. Free machining allows for maximum flexibility when sewing round the wire frame, so drop the teeth and use a darning foot.

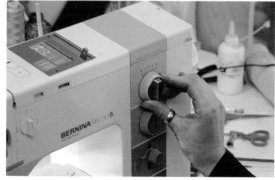

▶ *Setting stitch width dial*

◀ *Stitching wire frame to fabric*

Position the fabric with the wire frame placed under the machine foot, ready to stitch.
Start at one end of the frame and carefully stitch the wire into place – always keeping it in the middle of the machine foot.

Top tip Putting the needle in before turning tight corners gives you better control.

Using very sharp, small embroidery scissors, trim away the excess fabric. Be careful to not cut the stitches!

◀ *Trimming away excess fabric*

▶ *Putting a different colour spool in the machine*

Using two different coloured threads on the top reel and bottom spool creates variation in the petal edging. Here we've used green for the bottom thread and blue for the top one.

Sew tight zig-zag or satin stitches all the way round the wire petal outlines, completely covering the wire with thread.

Top tip   Stitching hand-sewing thread or wool to the edge of the petal will prevent frayed fabric from poking through the edging.

▶ *Edging petal*

◀ *Blanket stitching petals*

Cut a length of hand sewing thread which is long enough to allow you to blanket stitch all the way round the petals. Alternatively, try using different coloured threads at intervals if you're finding sewing with one long length tricky.

Start at the end of the petals and make a couple of stitches to secure the thread. Next, blanket stitch around the outline, always taking care to keep the stitches evenly spaced.

When you've blanket stitched all the petal 'fingers', stop stitching about 12 cm from the end of the wire. Then place the edges together to form a completely circular flower shape. Finish blanket stitching the two edges together – tying off with a couple of final stitches.

◀ *Sewing edges together using blanket stitch*

29

▶ *Sewing running stitch around bottom of petals*

Secure everything with a couple of stitches, and then sew a row of running stitches 1.5–2 cm from the bottom of the petals to gather them tight. Don't tie off – you'll need to tighten the stitches once you've added the middle of the flower.

You're now ready to make the flower centre.

To create the flower centre, fill the bobbin with shirring elastic.

Top tip   Hold the elastic with one hand while winding it on – this gives the elastic extra tension.

▶ *Placing shirring elastic on spool*

▼ *Placing lightweight fabric in embroidery ring*

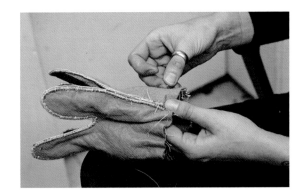

The middle of the flower is created by stitching in an increasing circle using shirring elastic – this gathers the fabric into a pod-like shape. This type of work is easiest if you use the darning foot.

The elastic is on the bottom bobbin, with a normal machine thread on the top. Set the machine to straight stitch, and with the teeth dropped, begin stitching in a small circle.

The thinner the fabric is, the tighter the shirring elastic will pull it together. Here we've used lightweight chiffon.

Working outwards from the centre, stitch to almost the edge of the ring. Remember to over-sew the last few stitches to prevent the work from becoming undone.

Pop the work out from the embroidery ring.

◀ *Increasing the circle's diameter*

The stem can be a single strand of wire, or can be doubled for extra strength. Bend the ends to avoid poking them through the fabric. Modelling wire is good for this task as it's particularly easy to manipulate, but garden wire works just as well.

If the fabric is transparent, stuff the stitched centre with the same fabric. Alternatively, try using glittery cut threads and wools for a more interesting combination. Place the stem in the middle of the flower centre and stuff the fabric evenly around it.

Make a couple of secure stitches, and then sew a line of running stitches across the bottom of the open 'pod' and pull tight.

▶ *Placing wire stem inside flower centre*

▼ *Enclosing the flower centre with thread*

▲ *Tying off the pod*

Wrap the thread around the stem and tie off.

Wrap thin gaffer tape or florists' tape around the base of the pod, and then work your way down the stem.

◀ *Wrapping thin gaffer tape or florists' tape round pod base*

 *Positioning centre inside the outer petals*

Position the flower centre inside the outer petals. The bottom of the petals will be joined just below where the flower centre meets the stem.

When the flower centre is in the desired position, pull the loose end of the running stitch you made earlier to gather the petals tightly and form the flower's main body.

Wrap the hand sewing thread around the base of the flower and pull tightly before tying off.

Cover the rough edges of the bottom of the flower with tape to conceal the stitch line. Then trim away any excess fabric to create a neat, even finish.

 *Wrapping hand sewing thread to secure petals*

▼ *Trimming away excess fabric*

▲ *Wrapping tape to cover join*

Continue wrapping with tape until the join between the flower head and stem is covered.

How much you gather the bottom of the flower body depends on how much material there is in the petals, and also on how big the centre 'pod' is.

◄ *Gathering fabric with hand stitches*

▶ *Embellishing with French knots*

Stab through the outer fabric and gather it into the 'pod'. Small jewellery pliers make it easier to pull a strong needle through thick fabric, so use a pair of these if possible.

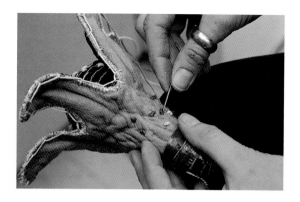

The small stab stitches where the fabric has been gathered can be disguised with decorative French knots, beads, small buttons or sequins.

To make French knots, insert needle at the point where you want the knot to be, and wrap the thread around the back of the needle at least twice – holding the yarn with your left thumb. Then, twist the needle back to the starting point and insert it close to where the thread first emerged. This will leave a small knot on the surface.

The flower centre can also be decorated in this way.

To finish your flower, wrap the whole stem in florists' tape. This comes in a variety of colours and is made from self-adhesive crêpe paper.

▲ *Wrapping stem with florists' tape to finish*

▶ *The finished flower*

33

4 Boil-away flowers

The flowers created in this project use many of the techniques demonstrated in the earlier chapter. The biggest difference is the introduction of hot-water-soluble (or 'boil-away') fabric, which allows the creation of a lace-type effect. Once you've stitched into this special fabric, building up a set of interlocking patterns, the background material gets dissolved in hot water – leaving just your stitching and any objects that you've stitched into the design.

TECHNIQUES |||||||||||||||||||||||||||||||

- Assembling a petal frame from wire
- Cutting
- Edging using satin stitch (machine stitch)
- Hand sewing
- Fabric manipulation
- Decorative French knots
- Wrapping tape

MATERIALS ||||||||||||||||||||||||||||||||

- Water soluble fabric
- Heat-fixed web adhesive or Bondaweb
- Scrap fabrics, leather off-cuts
- Plastic tubing, string, thin plastic cord, washing line
- Modelling wire or garden wire
- Electrical resistors with wire
- Hand and machine threads
- Thin gaffer tape or florists' tape
- Iron and ironing board
- Small beads
- Strong glue

▶ *Drawing template for flower petals*

Draw a template for the flower petals on to a piece of hot water soluble fabric, and place the work tightly into an embroidery ring.

Draw a series of interlinking swirls and loops inside the petal shape. These will guide you when stitching into the backing fabric.

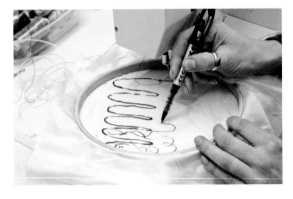

▶ *Drawing freehand patterns*

◀ *Stitching plastic cord into patterns on petal shapes*

Set the machine to a medium zig-zag stitch with the teeth dropped for free machine embroidery. Then, sew over the lengths of plastic cord (or string), making sure to join all ends together to form a mesh of interlocking loops – think of a spider's web if you need a mental image. (If you leave loose ends, the work will fall apart when the backing fabric gets dissolved.)

Set the machine to a straight or zig-zag stitch, and then fill in the petal shapes more densely with lots of stitches. Be sure to stitch over the plastic to create continuously linked or meshed patterns.

◀ *Filling in detail with stitch*

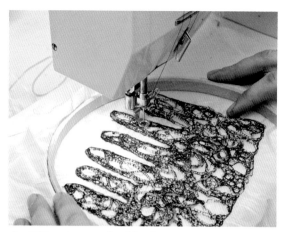

▲ *Filling in a mesh of finely stitched loops*

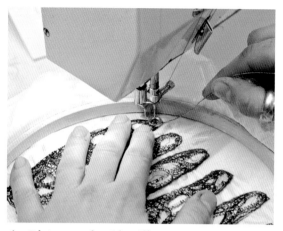

▲ *Edging petals with stiffening wire*

Set the machine to a zig-zag stitch with the teeth dropped, and then carefully sew the wire around the edge of the petal shapes.

Top tip   Be sure to catch the wire with the stitch so that the web of thread will hold together when the fabric dissolves.

Trim away the excess margins of the soluble fabric, and then boil a half-full pan of water and place the work in it (alternatively, use a kettle). Wait until all the backing fabric has dissolved, which should take about five minutes.

▲ *Placing work in pan of hot water to dissolve fabric*

▲ *Remove work from pan and drain*

▶ *Iron and flatten the work between clean cloths*

When the work has drained and cooled, lay it on a clean piece of cloth, put another piece of cloth on top, and iron to dry and press.

To give your flowers extra colour and texture, choose a backing fabric to place under the stitched mesh. Backing your petals in this way is an optional extra, but different fabrics with different weights will give the finished flowers lots of variety in look and feel. Here we've used a red velvet, though it's also worth considering fabrics which are lighter (such as silk) or coarser (such as hessian), which will also work well. Be experimental – in the past, we've even used cut-up plastic and metal scouring pads successfully!

▶ *Placing backing fabric behind the work and stitching*

◀ *Stitching the mesh on to the backing fabric*

Use a straight or zig-zag stitch to attach the mesh to the backing fabric, but be sure to use a zig-zag stitch to sew over the wire edges of the petals. When doing this, try to blend the new stitching over the stitches which are already in the mesh.

Trim carefully around the edge of the petals, making sure not to cut through the stitches that hold the wire in place.

◀ *Trimming away excess backing fabric*

▶ *Tidying up the edges with a zig-zag stitch*

With the machine still set to a zig-zag stitch, work all the way around the edge of the design to pull in the backing fabric and leave a neat edge.

Bring the right and left-hand edges of the petal together, and join them using either hand sewing or machine stitching.

▶ *Sewing the two end petals together to form a flower shape*

◀ *Drawing a design for the petal tips*

Another optional touch is adding detail to the tips of the petals. You can use a stiff fabric, plastic sheet or felt for this...almost any thin material with a bit of weight in it; here we've used thin coloured leather. To add this feature, place the material under the petal to gauge the size of the petal tip, and then draw an appropriate freehand shape.

To give even more interest to your petals, experiment with adding appliquéd shapes to the petal tips. Here we've used thin silver plastic sheet, bonded using an iron-on heat-fix adhesive web. All you have to do is draw the shapes on to the paper back of the adhesive web, and then cut them out.

◀ *Drawing a decorative shape on the back of heat-fixed adhesive web*

▲ *Cutting out decorative shapes to be bonded*

Next, peel the backing paper off the cut shapes and position them carefully on the drawn petal tips. Then, gently use the iron to bond them to the leather or backing fabric.

Using satin stitch, sew round the appliqué decoration on the petal tips. Then cut out each petal tip in preparation for it to be sewn to the main petals.

With your machine set to a zig-zag stitch, sew around the top curve of the petal to attach the tip.

▲ *Positioning decorative shapes on petal tips*

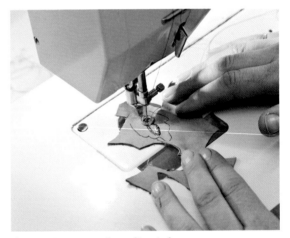

▲ *Sewing around appliqué shapes*

When you've made all your petals, turn back to the previous flower project to remind yourself how to make the flower centre 'pod' using fabric and shirring elastic.

▲ *Stitching petal tip on to flower*

▶ *Examples of finished flower petal rings*

After you've made the flower centre, the techniques for stuffing it and forming a wire stem are also the same as those shown in the previous chapter.

To create stamen filaments for the centre of your flowers, experiment with pipe cleaners and different types of wire. Whatever you choose, you need to cover them in stitch. Here we've filled the bottom spool with same multi-coloured thread as the top bobbin so that the stitch on the stamen filaments is matched and evenly coloured.

▶ *Winding multi-coloured thread on to the bottom spool*

◀ *Stitching on to electrical circuit components*

We used these little electrical circuit board components as the basis for our stamens. Dismantled electronic equipment can provide a treasure trove of tiny decorative objects for lots of craft projects.

Using a zig-zag stitch, carefully cover the wire.

Top tip   Hold the wire steady with one hand, using your other hand to keep the thread under tension so it doesn't get caught in the base plate slots.

◀ *Stitching over the resistor wires*

▶ *Bending the end of stamen wire with pliers*

Using small pliers, carefully bend one end of the stamen filament to form a tight loop. This loop forms the attachment point for the beads that make up the stamen's tip.

Using a fine needle, make a couple of small stitches through the loop and then thread several beads together. Next, catch them together to form a small cluster at the top of the stamen filament. To secure them, make a knot and tie off.

▶ *Hand-sewing beads on to tip of stamen*

◀ *Fixing loose threads with glue*

Using a thin glue such as textile glue or superglue, put tiny blobs on any loose ends of thread to stop them from unwinding.

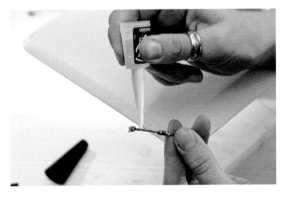

Make small holes in the finished flower centre pod with the sharp point of a small pair of scissors.

◀ *Making holes in flower centre pod for stamens*

To hold the stamen filaments in place, hand sew a couple of small stitches around the base of the stamen, and then decorate with French knots to hide the stitches. Instructions for making 'French knots' are given in the previous chapter.

Finish off your flower by assembling the centre pod and stem and then stitching them to the ring of petals. Details of the assembly process are covered in the previous project.

▶ *Securing stamens with decorative 'french knot' stitches*

▼ *Assembling the flower pod, stem and petals*

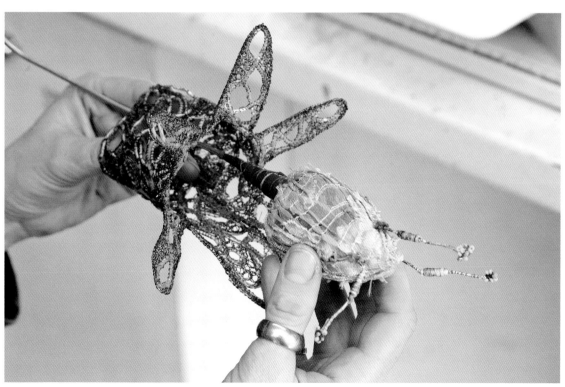

Finished flowers

5 Casting latex shapes

This workshop strays away from pure textiles a little, but learning the techniques of making moulds and casting latex will enable you to make small decorative objects which can be usefully incorporated into your textile and mixed media work.

Thin, colourful latex shapes can be cast from a huge range of everyday and natural objects. The objects you create can be sewn into your work, and also adapted as jewellery or fashion accessories.

TECHNIQUES |||||||||||||||||||||||||||||||||||||

- Preparing clay
- Mixing plaster
- Making a reusable plaster mould
- Mixing liquid latex

MATERIALS |||||||||||||||||||||||||||||||||||||||

- Objects to be cast (keep them simple at first)
- Clay
- Rolling pin
- Two flat sticks or battens
- Modelling plaster ('Plaster of Paris')
- Liquid latex
- Latex hardener
- Acrylic paint or dye
- 'Soft soap' (available from art or sculptural suppliers)

▶ *Preparing the clay*

Knead the clay to create a smooth lump with an even consistency throughout. This makes the clay more manageable and also removes air bubbles which could show up in the plaster mould.

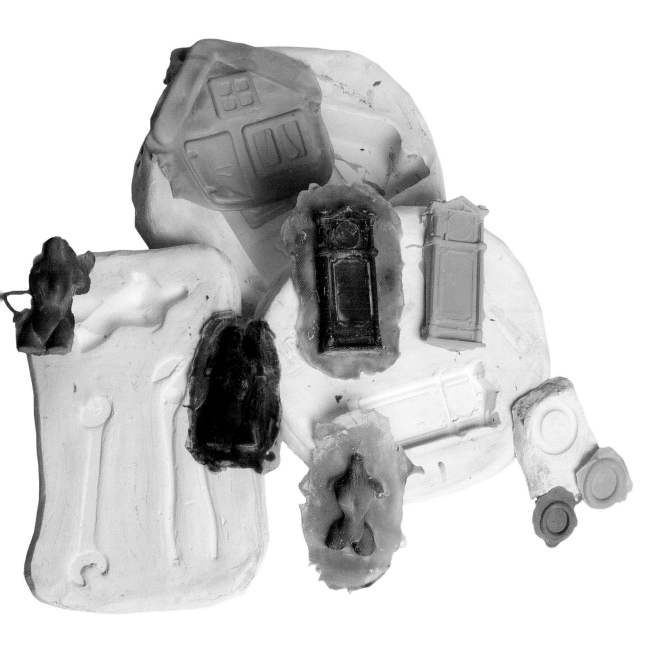

▶ *Rolling the clay flat between two wooden battens*

Cover the work surface with plastic to stop the clay from sticking, or alternatively place it on a board. Put a wooden batten on either side of the clay, too, as when you roll the clay out, these will ensure that you keep an even depth throughout. Before going further, also check that you've made the clay slab thick enough to insert your chosen object without it being pushed through to the work surface underneath.

Remove a thin area of surface clay so that you can press your chosen object into the clay slab. Allow for a 4–5 cm border of clay all around the object.

▶ *Scooping out some clay to position object*

▼ *Positioning object to be cast into the clay*

Top tip   Wind a bit of wire around the base of small objects such as buttons to make it easier to remove them after you've made a mould. You need to position the wired side of the object downwards into the clay slab at this stage for this to work.

Carefully position the object on the clay slab, and then press it down and smooth the clay up its edges. This prevents the poured plaster from seeping into gaps and ruining the mould.

Make sure that the clay is smooth around the object. A damp fine paintbrush can be used to seal the clay around the object if necessary.

◀ *Smoothing clay edges with paintbrush*

▶ *Positioning and smoothing clay edges*

If you want to cast multiple objects from one block of clay, remember to leave sufficient space between each object.

Smooth the clay around the base of the wall to make sure that it's securely fixed to the work surface.

Wipe the objects to be cast with a clean damp cloth to prevent bits of grit or clay from spoiling the mould.

▶ *Building a clay retaining wall around the slab*

▼ *Cleaning off excess clay from models*

▲ *Putting soft soap into a bowl*

Make up a 'soft soap' solution with a small amount of water in a dish, and then apply it with a soft cloth to the objects to be cast. This allows the plaster mould to be removed easily upon completion, and is called a 'release agent'.

◀ *Wiping soft soap solution on the objects to be cast*

49

▶ *Rubbing and sprinkling plaster into bowl of water*

Modelling plaster is always added to water; the amount of water that you need depends on the size of the object to be cast. Plaster goes off very quickly, so only mix the amount that you need for the job you're doing.

Pour some water into a bowl (warm water makes the plaster set faster). Sprinkle a handful of plaster evenly onto the surface of the water, rubbing it between your fingers; dumping in a whole lot of plaster prevents it from dispersing in the water and makes it very hard to achieve a smooth mixture.

Keep adding the plaster a handful at a time until it peaks above the surface of the water.

▶ *Mixing the plaster with the water*

▶ *Pouring the plaster mix into the mould tray*

Quickly mix the plaster until all the lumps are dispersed. Also, shake your fingers back and forth gently on the bottom of the bowl to help any air bubbles rise to the surface. When finished, the mixture should be smooth, and a little like a thick pancake mixture.

||||||||||||||||||||||||||||||||||||||||||||||||||||||||||||||||||||||||||||||||

Top tip   If you have any skin allergies or broken skin, wear thin disposable gloves for this procedure.

||||||||||||||||||||||||||||||||||||||||||||||||||||||||||||||||||||||||||||||||

Firmly banging the work surface with a rolling pin helps to disperse air bubbles while the plaster is still liquid.

Allow the plaster mould to set – a couple of hours in a warm room should do it. Then, carefully remove the clay wall so you can ease the mould away from the clay slab.

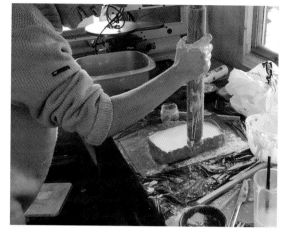

▲ *Banging work surface with rolling pin*

▲ *Peeling away the clay wall*

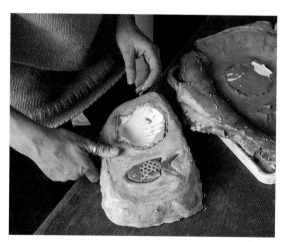

▲ *The plaster mould removed from the clay*

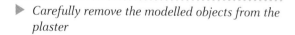

▶ *Carefully remove the modelled objects from the plaster*

When you've removed the casting models, allow the plaster to dry out completely. Leave it at least overnight – it's quite fragile until it's fully hardened off.

▶ *The mould ready to dry out*

When the mould is completely dry, carefully wipe away any clay residue with a clean, damp cloth.

Liquid latex is perfectly safe for most people to use, but it can cause an allergic skin reaction in others. If you know that you're one of these sufferers, remember to wear disposable non-latex gloves!

Mix enough liquid latex into a cup or small container to allow you to paint several layers on to your mould. It's also better to mix too little than too much.

◀ *Adding latex thickener to the liquid latex*

As a general guide, you need one part latex thickener to ten parts liquid latex. The thickener speeds up the drying time.

▶ *Pouring liquid latex into container*

Top tip   Work in a well-ventilated area so you won't be left with a rubbery pong after you've finished!

Both the liquid latex and the hardener are colourless, but dry to a dirty pale yellow. Adding water-based paints (acrylic is best), food colouring, inks or dyes will make your latex castings more attractive.

◀ *Adding colouring to the liquid latex*

▶ *Coating the mould with layers of liquid latex*

|||||||||||||||||||||||||||||||||||||||||||||||||||||||||||||||||||||||

Top tip   Swirling concentrated colouring into the latex solution creates interesting marbling effects. For an even colour, mix the colouring in thoroughly.

|||||||||||||||||||||||||||||||||||||||||||||||||||||||||||||||||||||||

Paint the latex on to the moulds, building it up in layers. Add a new layer when the previous one has dried - placing the mould on a cloth on a radiator will speed up this process. When you've finished, let the shapes dry completely before removing them from the moulds.

▶ *Coating the mould with layers of liquid latex*

▼ *The reusable mould with finished cast latex objects*

53

6 Mixed media panel

This workshop combines the moulding and casting techniques from the previous chapter with simple machine and hand stitching to create a picture story. We've made a simple hanging panel for this example, but you could create a picture to fit into a 3-D box frame like in the Story Boxes project later in this book.

Because the cast latex shapes are fairly thin and semi-translucent, this chapter could even be adapted to make functional textile structures such as lampshades and window blinds.

TECHNIQUES |||||||||||||||||||||||||||||||||||||||

- Planning and designing a picture
- Making a plaster mould (see Casting Latex Shapes)
- Casting liquid latex (see Casting Latex Shapes)
- Appliqué using heat-fix web adhesive
- Cutting
- Hand sewing
- Free machine embroidery

MATERIALS |||||||||||||||||||||||||||||||||||||||

- Latex shapes
- Scrap fabric, ribbon
- Dowel rods or thin garden canes
- Large beads for end-stops
- Glue
- Heat-fix web adhesive or Bondaweb
- Hand and machine sewing threads

Plan out the elements that will make up your picture story. Is it going to be a single frame, or perhaps cartoon-style with a series of frames that develop a narrative? Which parts of the picture will be cast, which stitched, and which formed from printed or appliquéd fabrics?

It's best to make thumbnail sketches to work out what goes where. Can you get away with using a single mould to make multiple images, or will you need to cast several different objects?

Take a large piece of plain calico or a pillowcase. Draw a simple frame to mark out your working area and then plan out your picture.

▲ *Sketchbook reference images*

Top tip   If you decide to use appliqué, numbering the different areas to be filled with fabric will make it easier to identify all the shapes you need.

Take a piece of heat-fix adhesive web and place it on your drawing with the paper backing side facing downwards. Then, carefully mark the sticky side with a felt pen. This will give you exact images of the shapes to be cut from fabric scraps for your appliqué.

▲ *Planning your picture layout*

▲ *Tracing out appliqué shapes on to heat-set web*

▶ *Cutting out adhesive-backed fabric shapes*

Turn the piece of web over and re-trace your lines on the paper side, and then bond your chosen fabrics to the sticky side of the web using an iron.

When you've prepared all your appliqué shapes, lay them carefully in position on the backing fabric. Cover with a clean cloth and iron to fix them.

▶ *Ironing on appliqué shapes*

◀ *Adding extra appliqué shapes*

Build up layers of appliquéd fabric shapes until you're happy with the result.

If you're unsure about how to make moulds, look back to the Casting Latex Shapes chapter. Then, cast the objects that you'll be adding to your picture.

If you plan to use multiple castings from a single mould, don't forget that you'll need several hours' setting time for each object before you can re-use the mould.

◀ *Peeling latex shapes away from moulds*

▶ *Marking positions of cast shapes*

Mark out the positions of your cast latex shapes on the fabric 'picture'. Don't trim away the excess rubber around the edges of your shapes yet!

Set the machine for free machine embroidery (teeth dropped, free machine embroidery or darning foot attached). Put the work into an embroidery ring and begin stitching into it to build up the picture.

Top tip   Work all the stitches in one area first, and only then reposition the ring.

▶ *Embroidering background details*

◀ *Sewing through a cast shape with decorative stitch*

Lay the latex shapes one at a time on to the fabric background. Use a small zig-zag stitch to secure the shape in position – zig-zag stitches are easiest because the latex is quite tricky to sew through, and they allow the machine to 'skip' stitches.

Once the shape is fixed into position, it's possible to add extra detail like the tree branches that are being stitched in here.

◀ *Carefully trim away excess latex from edges*

▲ *Adding extra stitched detail with coloured threads*

The cast latex shapes can be cut and manipulated to make interesting shapes. Here we've cut the centre out of a cast button to form a ring which will be stitched into the disc of our sun.

▶ *Cutting centre from a cast latex button to form a ring*

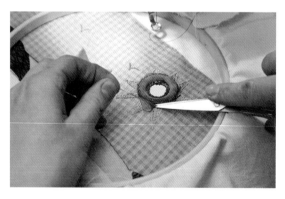

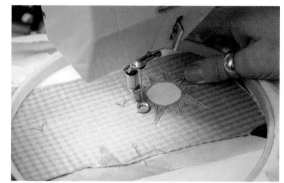

◀ *Cutting away excess latex after shape is secured*

Stitch the cast shape into the background fabric, and then trim away any excess latex as before.

Top tip   Using a dark thread helps to outline the different elements of your composition and makes them stand out from the background.

◀ *Edging the sun with a black stitch outline*

Hand-sewing stitches can be used to highlight areas or add detail. Try using different weights of thread and different stitches for variation (French knots, running stitch, cross stitch etc.).

Raise the teeth on your sewing machine, and also attach a standard straight stitch or zig-zag foot. Then, attach a decorative strip of fabric or ribbon along the bottom of the panel with straight or small zig-zag stitches.

Top tip   Edge the end of the panel with a zig-zag stitch while it's laid out flat to avoid it fraying when you cut excess fabric away later.

The ribbon trim is both decorative and functional. By turning the ribbon back on itself and re-sewing along the stitch line, you create a casing in which to insert the hanging rod.

Top tip   Make sure the casing is wide enough for the rod to be inserted!

Attach a decorative strip of fabric or ribbon along the top of the panel in the same way as you did for the bottom strip.

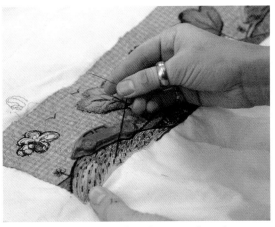

▲ *Adding detail with hand-sewing threads*

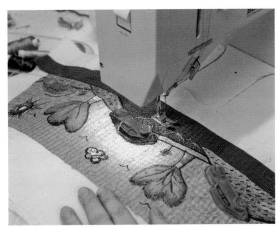

▲ *Attaching a ribbon along the bottom of the hanging*

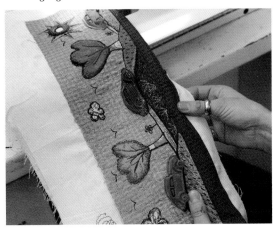

▲ *Turning the ribbon under to create a casing*

▶ *Attaching a ribbon along the top of the hanging*

Form a decorative casing to insert the top hanging rod as before.

▲ *Attaching a ribbon along the top of the hanging*

▲ *Machining along the top ribbon strip*

▲ *Turning the ribbon under to create a casing*

Trim away excess fabric from both sides of the panel.

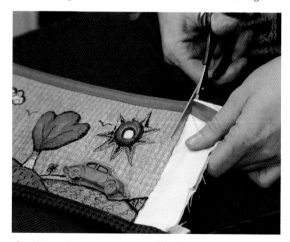

▲ *Trimming away excess fabric*

▶ *Trimming away excess fabric from back of panel*

To avoid bulky backing, trim away any excess fabric from the back of the panel. Be sure to leave a couple of centimetres of material from the ribbon overhang.

Cut a piece of decorative fabric for your backing panel – leaving a 1 cm seam allowance all the way round. Turn and iron the seam allowance under, and then pin or bond the fabric in place. With the machine's teeth raised and a normal foot attached, sew the backing panel in place.

||||||||||||||||||||||||||||||||||||||||||||||||||||||||||||||||||||||||||||

Top tip   You'll get a neater finish if you do this from the front of the panel.

||||||||||||||||||||||||||||||||||||||||||||||||||||||||||||||||||||||||||||

▶ *Bonding decorative fabric to back of panel*

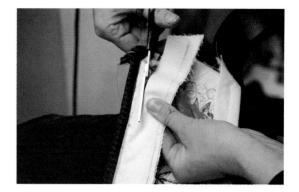

◀ *Cutting dowel or garden cane to required length*

Put the dowel rods or thin garden canes in place, and cut them to the desired length – either with a small craft saw or a pair of sharp pliers. Leave the rods protruding by about an inch on either side of the casing.

To prevent the panel from slipping, glue on large beads as end-stops or wrap ribbon around the ends of each rod.

◀ *Putting glue on the ends of the rods*

61

▶ *Attaching decorative rosettes with hand-sewing thread*

We added small rosettes at opposite corners of the hanging for extra emphasis. Now, just tie a strand of thin ribbon to both ends of the top rod and your panel is ready to hang on a wall!

▲ *The finished panel*

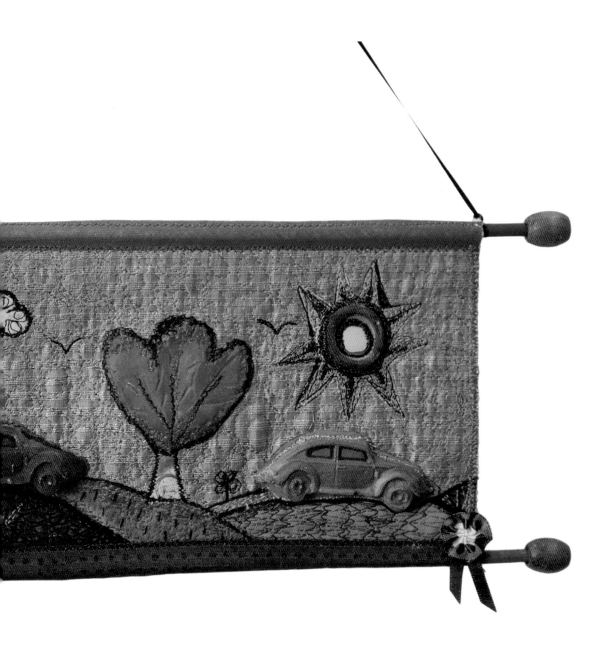

7 Bird

This chapter fuses textile techniques with sculptural forms to create a 3-D model. We've chosen to model a bird because its wings, plumage and tail can be replicated using the textile techniques that you've learnt through this book. Fish, insects, fairies, angels or mythical creatures like dragons and griffins would also make good subjects.

TECHNIQUES |||||||||||||||||||||||||||||||||||

- Designing and drawing a bird
- Creating an armature
- Making papier maché
- Painting
- Cutting
- Free machine embroidery
- Appliqué

MATERIALS ||||||||||||||||||||||||||||||||||

- ▶ Modelling wire
- ▶ Florists' wire decorations
- ▶ Pliers
- ▶ Gaffer tape
- ▶ Old newspapers
- ▶ PVA glue
- ▶ Paints and varnish
- ▶ Heat-fix web adhesive or Bondaweb
- ▶ Scrap fabrics
- ▶ Hand and machine threads
- ▶ Iron and ironing board
- ▶ Small beads, recycled jewellery
- ▶ Beading needles, hand sewing needles

Research the imagery for your subject. For a bird, look carefully at how wings, feathers, tails etc. appear in nature. Try to look under the plumage, too: what holds the bird together? How does it perch or stand? This will help you visualise how to construct your armature – the basic framework or 'skeleton' for the model.

When you've planned your basic skeleton, make a shape to form the bird's body. We've used a polystyrene ball – expanded polystyrene can be cut from packaging material or bought at craft shops, and it's easy to shape with a craft knife. Alternatively, you can use flower-arrangers' 'oasis' block. These materials are dense enough to provide support, but lightweight and soft enough to stick modelling wire into.

It's best to use heavier modelling wire to form the basic skeleton before progressing on to lighter weights to work on more detailed areas like the beak, claws and body.

Top tip   Thin modelling wire is easier to bend and twist, and so gives more precise control for doing delicate work

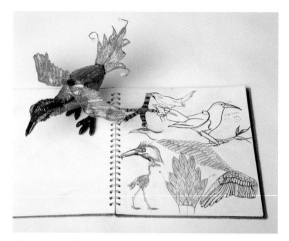

▲ *Research*

▲ *Building up armature in soft modelling wire*

▲ *The finished armature*

Tear up plenty of newspapers into small scraps and add hot water until you get a paste. Keep stirring until all the water is absorbed and the paper fibres 'relax' – you're looking to end up with a thick, heavy, gooey mulch which looks a bit like porridge.

Next, slowly add PVA liquid adhesive until the mixture is evenly covered.

Work the papier maché into the bird's body, neck and head. Putting a blob of PVA in the palm of your hand will help you to smooth the pulp over the armature more easily – watch out for sharp wire ends when doing this, though!

Pour half a cupful of PVA adhesive into a shallow container (e.g. an old ice cream tub). Then, tear up some thin strips of newspaper – about the size of a standard ruler is fine, with some thinner ones for detail work.

These strips will then be dipped into PVA to produce paper 'bandages' which you can wrap round the mulched body.

Top tip   Stick the bird's feet to a chopping board with gaffer tape. This will stop the model from toppling over while you're working, and also allow you to work at different angles by turning the board around.

Papier maché mulch can be manipulated like clay, particularly when it's starting to dry out. Good effects include flicking the prongs of a fork over the body to simulate plumage and 'drawing' into the surface with the point of a pencil to create details such as eyes.

▲ *Making papier maché mulch*

▲ *Pouring PVA adhesive into a separate container*

▲ *Building up body detail*

▶ *Prime the bird's body with white emulsion to seal it*

When you've added surface detail to the papier maché, let the bird dry out completely. When this is done, prime the body with emulsion paint – this gives a sealed, uniform surface for the top coats of paint.

Using acrylic or water-based paints and a range of brush sizes, decorate the bird. When you're happy with the overall result, finish the job with a couple of coats of varnish.

▶ *Painting body detail*

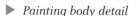

◀ *Drawing wing and tail templates*

Sketch out the wings and tail, making sure that you've got the scale right and that the shapes you choose will fit the bird's body. Don't forget that you need a right wing and a left wing – draw one, then turn it over and trace it to create a mirror image.

Iron a piece of heat-fix adhesive web on to the back of your chosen fabric. We chose thin transparent chiffon, as this allowed us to trace the tail and wing designs from our sketches straight on to the fabric. If you decide to use a heavier fabric, make card templates from your sketches and use these to transfer your designs on to the fabric.

◀ *Tracing tail on to chiffon backed with heat-fix web*

▲ *Tracing wing onto chiffon*

▲▼ *Adding further appliqué detail to wings*

You need to put the wing panels and tail on to a large, thin piece of backing fabric which can be secured in an embroidery ring, because you'll be stitching them later. Again, we used heat-set web for this.

To create detail on the tail and wings, try using different fabrics for different parts of the plumage. Trace around the area you want to highlight, then transfer the shape on to the fabric backed with heat-set web. Cut out the shapes neatly, position them carefully, and iron to fix them.

Set the machine for free machine embroidery – drop the teeth and attach a darning or free machine embroidery foot. Using a combination of straight and zig-zag stitches for variety, stitch through and round the appliqué detail shapes to fix them permanently and add decorative detail.

The underside of the wings and tail will also be visible when your bird is finished, so give some thought to the kind of effect you want to create.

Top tip   Try placing a different colour of fabric underneath, or use different colour threads on the two bobbins.

▶ *Stitching into the wing*

▶ *Stitching wire stiffening around edge of wing*

The edges of the wing and tail panels need stiffening – wire gives them strength and structure, and also allows you to position them. You can use heavy electrical wire stripped from cable, gardening wire or even pipe cleaners for this.

Set the machine to a medium zig-zag stitch and position the foot directly over the wire so that alternate stitches fall either side of the wire and secure it in place. Make sure the wire doesn't get dragged down through the hole on the bed plate – hold it fairly taut in one hand as you stitch and only go slowly so as to stay in control.

▶ *Trimming excess fabric from the wing*

◀ *Edging and tidying up a wing*

With the machine set to a medium zig-zag stitch, re-sew the edges of the wings and tail to catch frayed edges and loose threads. You can use a contrasting thread to pick out the feather shapes, or even metallic or multi-coloured threads for more variety.

After you've edged the tail, sew some equally spaced wire 'quills' in to the work. This creates the look of large tail feathers and also has a structural function – it allows you to adjust the tail to fit the back end of your bird.

Top tip   Leave wires projecting from the tail; these can be pushed into the bird's body to attach the tail.

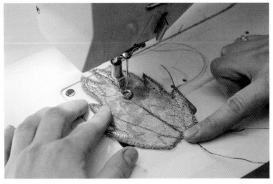

◀ *Sewing wire strengthening 'quills' in to tail panel*

▶ *Adding florists' beaded wire decorations*

Florists' accessories can add extra shape and interest to almost any textile work. Here we stitched some beaded wires on to the tail feathers.

Position the tail carefully on the back end of the bird's body, and then mark the places where the securing wires need attaching.

The wings can be secured using a similar technique to the tail: we used a single heavy wire that pierced the inner ends of both wings and went into the body of the bird. To finish it off, we fixed a big, ruby-like bead to the end of the wire.

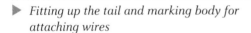

▶ *Fitting up the tail and marking body for attaching wires*

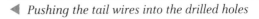

◀ *Drilling holes in bird's body for securing wires*

Using a drill with a very fine bit or a small bodkin, pierce the bird's body where you marked the positions for the attaching wires.

Push the attaching wires gently but firmly into the holes that you drilled in the bird's rear end.

◀ *Pushing the tail wires into the drilled holes*

▶ *Gluing the attached tail for extra strength*

Using a strong, runny glue, carefully put a blob on each wire at the point where it enters the bird. This will help to stop the wires from pulling out of the body after completion.

Your bird won't moult and doesn't need feeding

The small bird created in this project might give you some ideas for bigger and more complex textile sculptures. This fantastical griffin bird, for example, was designed to hang from a chain, and is over four feet long with a wingspan of six feet. The body is an agricultural drum covered with chicken wire and papier maché. Strips of individually stitched feathers were wrapped around the body, then pinned and glued; a similar technique was used for the tail. The head, body, tail and feet were all made as separate elements so the sculpture could be dismantled for transportation.

▼ *And here's one we did earlier!*

8 Heads

How far you push the boundaries of textile art is limited only by your imagination and the extent to which you can use materials and technologies.

The craft is particularly enjoyable, too, because of how hugely rewarding it can be to turn an idea and a couple of working sketches into something you can touch, feel and manipulate. The heads created here were all made using easily accessible materials and by combining simple modelling techniques with hand and machine stitching.

TECHNIQUES

- Making templates for fabric cutting
- Assembling armatures/frameworks from scrap materials
- Fabric painting
- Cutting
- Machine and hand sewing
- Sticking
- Using wire for stiffening

MATERIALS

- Soft leather pieces (gloves, chamois leather)
- Fabric scraps
- Fabric paints
- Beads, buttons
- Felting fibres or wool (for hair)
- Hand sewing threads
- Iron and ironing board
- Fabric glue or heat gun
- PVA adhesive
- ModRoc ('Plaster of Paris' bandage)
- Old newspapers (for papier maché)
- Gaffer tape
- Junk materials to make body armatures (cardboard, old bottles, large bobbin reels)
- Modelling or garden wire, pipe cleaners

Courtesy of Sue Macdonald

Courtesy of Samantha Bryan

▲ *Reference source material*

To get some ideas for this project, you really need to take a long look at heads. You could start by looking in the mirror or taking pictures of a friend or family member, or maybe even by sketching some cartoon characters of your own. Alternatively, look at art reference books, postcards and online galleries to see how artists deal with the shapes and features that make every human unique. Stylised images are particularly fun to work with – anything from manga to Modigliani – and don't forget ethnic art, folk art, masks, theatre, dolls, puppetry or the huge range of inspirational sculpture, either.

▶ *Drawing around the template for the head*

Draw a template for the head shape on paper or card, and then transfer it on to a piece of chamois leather or glove material.

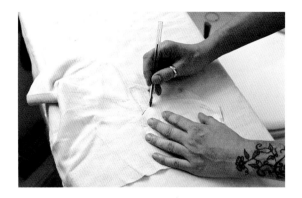

▶ *Laying heat-fixed web adhesive to back of face*

◀ *Laying bonded face to background cloth*

Cut out the leather face and then bond it to a piece of lightweight background cloth that will fit into an embroidery ring.

Mark the facial features, and glue or heat-fix fabric highlights for cheeks, lips, beauty spots etc.

◀ *Attaching detail to face*

▶ *Trimming finger of glove*

The finger of an old glove makes a great nose
shape – just cut it away from the rest of the glove,
and snip down a seam to splay it out.

▶ *Splaying out finger of glove*

◀ *Drawing on nose shape*

Draw the nose lines and the desired nose shape.

Trim away the excess leather around your nose
outline.

◀ *Trimming away excess leather*

▶ *Embroidering on nose lines*

Position the nose on thin fabric in an embroidery ring. Set the machine to a free machine embroidery stitch by dropping the teeth, and then machine along the marked lines; satin stitching at a Number 2 setting should give a good result.

|||||||||||||||||||||||||||||||||||||||||||||||||||||||||||||||||||||||||||||||||||||

Top tip   Glue or bond the nose to the fabric to make sure it stays in place when you're stitching.

|||||||||||||||||||||||||||||||||||||||||||||||||||||||||||||||||||||||||||||||||||||

Remove the sewn nose from the ring and trim away excess fabric, carefully snipping close to the stitches.

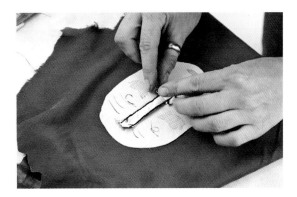

▶ *Cutting away excess leather*

▶ *Placing nose on face*

Position the nose on the face, and then, using a straight stitch, sew along the satin stitched edge. This creates a casing which you can later stuff to give the nose a 3-D look – as well as attaching the nose to the face.

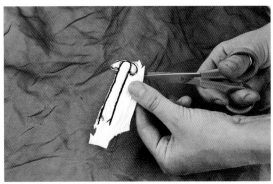

▶ *Sewing embroidered lines around the outline*

Facial hair can simply be machine stitched straight on. Our very hairy man has felting fibres for his hair, eyebrows and moustache, but you could also use wool or cut threads.

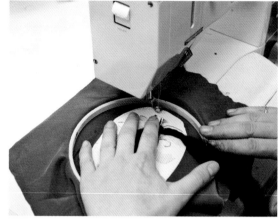

▲ *Adding eyebrows*

Pipe cleaners at the ends of his handlebar moustache add shape and prevent drooping! To add these, set the machine to a zig-zag stitch, take the work out of the ring, and fold back the backing fabric so it's not in the way. Overlay the pipe cleaner on to the felting fibre, and stitch several times to secure it. Next, cut to the desired length using small electrical pliers or jewellery cutters.

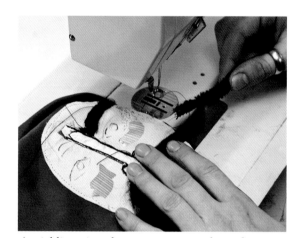

▲ *Adding pipe cleaners to moustache ends*

A good way to create eyelids is to cut thin strips of fabric or leather and position them around the eyes, stitching with either a zig-zag or a straight stitch according to your preference. Our man had his eyes worked into with satin stitch several times over to give the illusion of stump work (a raised embroidery effect on a fabric background).

Facial details such as shading and eye colouring need to be stitched in at this stage using a combination of coloured threads and free machine embroidery.

▲ *Forming eyelids in leather*

Solid areas of shading can be built up using straight stitch with the teeth dropped and a free machine embroidery foot fitted.

When you've finished embroidering the face, cut a small slot through the reverse of the backing fabric where the nose is.

▲ *Cutting slot through backing material*

Carefully use the point of a small pair of scissors to force kapok, cotton wool or similar fine stuffing material through the slot. Stitch up the slot when the desired degree of 'nose-ness' has been achieved.

▲ *Stuffing the nose through slot in back*

Stitching stretchy fabric all the way around the face makes it easy to attach it to a head form later on. Here this is being done in sections, seamed roughly at each section joint. We used old opaque tights around the face and a matching chamois leather strip under the chin, as this part will be visible on the finished head.

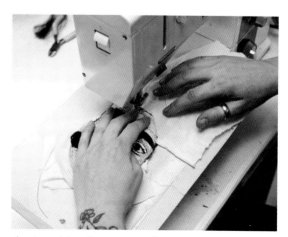

▲ *Attaching face to stretchy material*

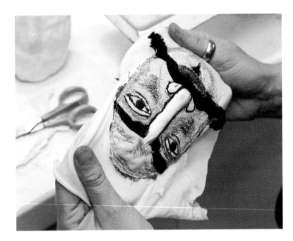

◀ *Completed face ready to attach to armature*

The head form or 'armature' can be made using a variety of materials.

Here we made it from a tightly rolled-up ball of newspaper. Be sure to make a hole in the centre of the ball with your thumb, as this is where the head will eventually fit on to the neck. When you have the shape, wind gaffer tape and ModRoc tightly around the structure to build it up.

▲ *Making head armature from paper, tape and ModRoc*

Smooth several layers of ModRoc over the head to finish off. Allow to dry (a couple of hours in a warm oven should do the job). If enough layers of ModRoc are added over a moistened newsprint ball, the newsprint can be removed from the centre of the head once the outside is dry, and the head will keep its shape while remaining pliable for a while longer. This allows further manipulation, letting you fine-tune the shape and also sew through after you stretch material over the armature.

▲ *Smoothing off the head shape*

Stretch several layers of fabric over the head shape – the feet of tights or old socks work particularly well.

||||||||||||||||||||||||||||||||||||||||||||||||||||||||||||||||||||||||||||||||||||||||

Top tip   Tie a knot at the top of the head – this makes it easier to attach hair.

||||||||||||||||||||||||||||||||||||||||||||||||||||||||||||||||||||||||||||||||||||||||

Head armatures can be made out of a variety of materials: finials from curtain poles come with necks attached; polystyrene is easy to cut to shape; and the ModRoc/papier maché combo gives you total control. Alternatively, you could experiment with dense sponge, an old tennis ball on a stick, or forming chicken wire over rags or newsprint.

Whatever you use to form your head, encasing it in stretchy fabric gives you a surface on which you can stitch the face, hair, ears, headgear and so on.

▲ *Covering head with stretch fabric*

▲ *Tie a knot at top of head*

Place the flat face in the palm of one hand with the head structure on top. Next, make a secure stitch in the fabric on the back of the head armature, and then stitch through the surrounding fabric on the flat face. Work evenly around the face, stretching and sewing a small section at a time so the face is taut. It might help to pin the work, adjusting the tautness as you sew.

▲ *Positioning flat embroidered face over armature*

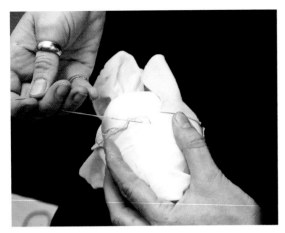

▲ *Sewing face to armature*

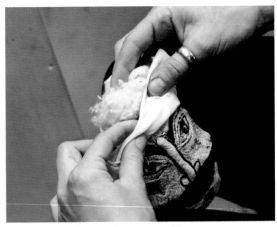

▲ *Shaping face with extra stuffing*

The stitches will be concealed in the hair, so use double thread and really stretch the face to the head form with big stitches and a thick needle.

You can add padding between the layers to build up the face structure – making a prominent chin, big lips, cheekbones, forehead etc.

||||||||||||||||||||||||||||||||||||||||||||||||||||||||||||||||||||||||||||||||

Top tip   Fine jewellery pliers can make it easier to pull the needle through, if necessary.

||||||||||||||||||||||||||||||||||||||||||||||||||||||||||||||||||||||||||||||||

▲ *Head ready to be attached to body*

▶ *Once the face is attached to the head, it's easy to add more fine detail with fabric paint*

Like the head, a body armature can be created from a collection of materials: plastic bottles, large thread or wool bobbins, small kitchen funnels, cardboard tubes etc. (If you use a plastic bottle, it can be filled with rice or sand to make for a really stable, free-standing body.)

Here's a body armature made from a large, empty wool spool with thin strips of MDF taped to the body to form a neck. Alternatively, a neck could be already attached to the head, as with curtain finials. If a body tube is used, however, this must be narrow enough to fit inside the neck opening.

Here the neck forms part of the body and the head will be placed on top.

As with the head form, the body armature can be built up using papier maché, gaffer tape and ModRoc.

Whether the body is made from smoothed ModRoc or papier maché, features like breasts, bums and bellies can be added as you build up the structural shape.

To make the model lifelike, use the same material to form a neck tube – cut a rectangle, fold it in half and stitch along the long side. Then, turn it through and glue it into place.

▲ *Creating body armature*

▲ *Adding body bumps*

▲ *Covering neck with flesh coloured tubing*

85

To make a suit or covering, place right sides of fabric together, then draw around the body shape. Be sure to leave a bit extra (1–1.5 cm) for seam allowance and manoeuvring.

Cut out, pin, sew and turn through; details can be glued or stitched on afterwards. If stitching, first bond the fabrics into place on the right side of one piece of fabric, and then stitch before pinning and sewing the two sides together.

Collar and lapels can now be added. Cut a strip of fabric, then fuse a strip of interfacing which is half the width of the fabric on the wrong side – like the jam in a sandwich. This interfacing adds stiffness.

Fold the fabric in half and place around the neck. Draw the lapel shape, then sew along the pen lines.

Cut away excess fabric, and then use a zig-zag stitch to neaten the edges – also saving the need to turn it through.

The hairy man's neck and head are formed like a ball and socket joint so his head can be posed in a variety of positions. This sort of joint allows for much greater and more lifelike flexibility.

▲ *Use body as a template to cut clothing patterns*

▲ *Adding details to outfit*

▲ *Marking out lapels on suit*

The neck is simply wound round at the end with fabric, and then neatened and secured with gaffer tape. Aim for a snug, friction fit to avoid ending up with a wobbly head.

Hair can be pattern cut by placing fabric or tissue paper on the head and creating a pattern to be assembled in sections. This can then be stitched to the head through the stretchy fabric afterwards.

The easiest way to do this is to use wool or felting fibres which can then be glued or stitched to the scalp in sections.

Top tip   Tying a knot at one end of each strand allows the hair to be stitched at the roots. When all the hair is attached, trim away the excess to create a hairstyle.

Ears can be added last so they don't get in the way when attaching the hair.

Draw a matching pair using the same material that the face and neck were made from, adding flaps so they can be stitched or glued to the sides of the head.

Top tip   Edging the ears with soft wire allows them to be manipulated after you've attached them.

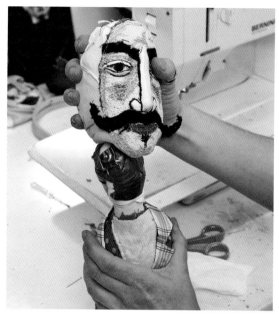

▲ *Placing head on body*

▲ *Attaching hair*

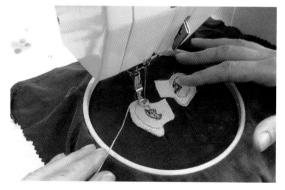

▲ *Creating ears*

▲ *Hirsute man*

THE HENLEY COLLEGE LIBRARY

▲ *Freaky females and spare faces*

9 Story boxes

This chapter uses stitches to 'draw' and 'paint' two-dimensional images that can become characters in a three-dimensional 'story box'. Collaged or montaged images form the background. These can be drawings, paintings, postcards, sweet papers, scraps, cut-ups, old storybooks or cartoons – in fact, anything that can be pasted to a background.

You might like to look at Victorian model theatres, puppet theatres, pop-up books and even religious artefacts like altar-pieces for inspiration. Alternatively, just type 'story box' into Google to see how other artists have used similar ideas.

TECHNIQUES

- Tracing and transferring imagery onto fabric
- Cutting and assembling
- Free machine embroidery
- Painting and découpage backgrounds for boxes
- Cutting wood blocks
- Sanding and gluing
- Assembling

MATERIALS

- Variety of fabrics
- Heat-fixed web adhesive or Bondaweb
- Leather, thin vinyl or stiffened non-fraying fabric
- Machine thread
- Foam board or thick mounting card
- Wood for blocks
- Acrylic paints
- Scrap book images for découpage
- Varnish
- Iron and ironing board

▶ Tracing sketch or design onto fabric

Make outlines or sketches of your character or characters on paper. Keep your designs bold and simple. Next, transfer the image(s) on to the middle of an ironed piece of calico, making sure to use a piece of fabric which is large enough to fit securely into an embroidery ring.

Top tip   Use a light box (or tape the drawing and the fabric to a window when it's sunny) to make a clear copy of your original sketch.

Decide where you want to add extra detail or emphasis to the character using appliqué. This figure will have her hair and clothes appliquéd in striped pink silk.

▲ Tracing outline of hair on to heat-fixed web adhesive

◀ Ironing web adhesive to back of fabric

Using a felt pen, trace the parts of the image that will be appliquéd on to the sticky side of a piece of heat-fixed web adhesive (or Bondaweb). Doing it this way means that everything will be the right way round when you iron the design to the appliqué material.

Next, iron the traced design on to the back of the appliqué silk with the adhesive side facing down.

Cut out the bonded fabric along the drawn outlines and peel off the backing paper.

Position all the first layer of appliqué (e.g. hair, jacket), and then iron to fix to the base calico.

◀ Positioning appliqué hair on to base calico

Top tip   If you're using delicate fabrics, put
          a clean piece of cloth on the work
          before ironing.

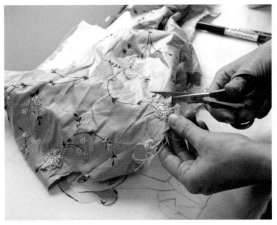

▲ *Cutting flowers out of decorative fabric*

To add further detail, choose fabrics with interesting prints or textures, or even use scraps of embroidery. Fix these with heat-fix web in the same way as the hair and jacket, creating an extra layer of appliqué.

Cheeks, lips, eyes etc. can also be added in fabrics – though this character will have her highlights and details added in stitch.

While you're cutting and bonding, decide which elements in the backdrop of your story box will be created in fabrics. Think about the scale and perspective of your background images, and also the way they're going to relate to your foreground character(s).

▲ *Appliquéd head and body ready to sew*

The backdrop for this story box is buildings. These houses are partly drawn on plain fabric and partly bonded shapes cut from printed fabric, appliquéd in the same way as our principal character.

▲ *Bonding fabrics to calico to create houses*

With the machine set to free machine embroidery (teeth dropped and with the darning foot or free machine embroidery foot fitted), begin to embroider the shading.

Three colours of flesh tones have been used for this character. Look at paintings or photographs to see where to put areas of shade or light. Use a pale thread to create highlights for areas such as cheekbones, brows, the bridge of the nose and eye sockets.

| | | | | | | | | | | | | | | | | | | | | | | | | | | | | | | | | | | | | | | | | | | | | | | | | | | | | | | | | | | | | | | | | | | | | | | | | | | | | | | | | | | | | | | | |

Top tip   Stitch all areas in one colour before switching threads.

| | | | | | | | | | | | | | | | | | | | | | | | | | | | | | | | | | | | | | | | | | | | | | | | | | | | | | | | | | | | | | | | | | | | | | | | | | | | | | | | | | | | | | | | |

Use black stitch lines just like you'd use a pen to give strong definition to eyes, lips, nostrils and so on.

Pop the stitched character out of the ring and loosely trim away the excess fabric.

Iron heat-fix web adhesive on to the back of the image, and then carefully cut away the excess fabric close to the machine stitches.

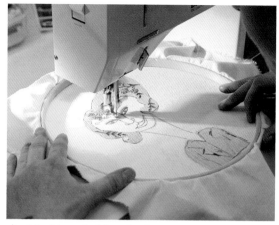

▲ *Machine stitching the face*

▲ *Adding finishing touches to machine embroidered face*

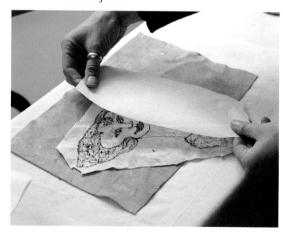

▲ *Placing heat-fix web adhesive on the back of the image*

▲ *Fixing the image to the leather backing with the iron*

. . . .

Use an iron to mount the work on leather or a stiffened backing which won't fray.

Machine sew to secure everything, making sure that frayed edges are sewn over.

. . . .

▼ *Tracing template onto foam board*

▲ *Head ready to be attached to mount board*

. . . .

Then, cut away the excess backing, leaving 0.5 cm edging all the way round.

Foam board or thick card is ideal for mounting your character(s) – both are lightweight and durable. Trace a template slightly smaller than the actual figure on to the mounting material.

▲ *Cutting out foam board template with craft knife*

▲ *Gluing foam board to the reverse of the figure*

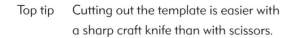

||||||||||||||||||||||||||||||||||||||||||||||||||||||||||||||||||||||||||||||||

Top tip   Cutting out the template is easier with a sharp craft knife than with scissors.

||||||||||||||||||||||||||||||||||||||||||||||||||||||||||||||||||||||||||||||||

Glue the foam board template to the back of the embroidered figure with either a glue gun or a strong contact adhesive.

▲ *Mounted image ready to be fixed to block*

Assemble your imagery for the other background elements – trees, houses, grass, hedges etc. Cut the images out with small scissors or a craft knife, and then montage them using spray adhesive, rubber solution or a glue stick.

||||||||||||||||||||||||||||||||||||||||||||||||||||||||||||||||||||||||||||||||

Top tip   Don't use PVA glue, as it tends to wrinkle thin paper.

||||||||||||||||||||||||||||||||||||||||||||||||||||||||||||||||||||||||||||||||

▶ *Cutting scrap images for decoupage*

Cut your backdrop montage to fit inside the back of your chosen display box.

There are plenty of choices when it comes to sourcing story boxes; big home décor stores sell display boxes in various sizes which usually have glass or acrylic glazing, or you can adapt an old wooden tray, a seed box, a shallow fruit box or even a small drawer. It's quite easy to find lightweight perspex or an acrylic sheet which can be cut to fit the front of your story box, then taped or glued into position to seal the finished work.

It's best to paint your display box inside and out, but remember that wooden boxes will need priming before you paint or decorate them. The box itself could form part of the artwork, too – for instance, your character could be looking out of a window in a fairytale tower. The box then becomes the stage on which your character's story is played out.

You can add all sorts of interesting effects to your story box. Here we've sanded it lightly with fine-grained sandpaper to give an appearance of age.

Once you've finished preparing your story box, give it a good shake or dust down before sticking your backdrop in. When the glue has dried, finish it by sealing it with a coat of matt or satin varnish.

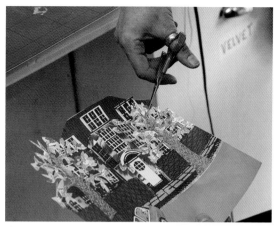

▲ *Trimming the montaged backdrop*

▲ *Sanding the painted story box to add 'age' and texture*

▲ *Sticking backdrop into painted box*

Cut a small piece of wood to make a 'stand up' block for each object in your box.

▲ *Mounting figure on 'stand up' block*

Using a glue gun or strong adhesive, stick 'stand up' blocks to the bottom of each object and allow them to dry fully.

▲ *Gluing 'stand up' block to mounted figure*

Experiment with the best positions for each character or object in the box. When you're happy with the overall effect, glue the base of each stand-up block into position.

▲ *Positioning objects in box*

▲ *The finished story box – Sally in Suburbia*

10 Dead cosy

For this project, we created a totally over-the-top and wildly kitsch tea cosy. You can choose any inspiration for the decoration of your project, but we've chosen the Mexican 'Day of the Dead' (*Diá de los Muertos*), which is celebrated with dolls, paintings, statues and even sweets that depict symbols of mortality such as skulls and skeletons!

TECHNIQUES ||||||||||||||||||||||||||||||||||||||

▷ Making a paper pattern template
▷ Cutting
▷ Edging using satin stitch (machine stitch)
▷ Free machine embroidery
▷ Hand sewing
▷ Fabric manipulation
▷ Piping and edging
▷ Appliqué (using heat-fixed web adhesive)

MATERIALS |||||||||||||||||||||||||||||||||||||||

▷ Heat-fixed web adhesive or Bondaweb
▷ Scrap fabrics, silks, fake fur trim, lace doily or antique lace
▷ Plastic tubing, string, thin plastic cord, washing line or piping cord
▷ Wadding
▷ Hand and machine threads
▷ Iron and ironing board
▷ Decorative buttons
▷ Elastic thread

▶ *Reference material and design sketches*

Find suitable reference material for the decorative imagery you wish to put on the cosy. We used our own sketches, gardening books for the flower references, images from the internet and some authentic Mexican memorabilia.

▶ *Measuring teapot to gauge dimensions of tea cosy*

Measure your teapot – width and height – to decide how big your pattern template for the cosy needs to be. Add at least 3–4 cm to each dimension so the final fit isn't too snug.

Measure the width and height on to a piece of card or paper, and then draw a roughly semi-circular outline for the pattern template.

▶ *Drawing an outline for the template*

◀ *The finished paper template*

Lay the paper template on to your chosen piece of fabric with a piece of wadding of the same size placed underneath. Here we've chosen a piece of scrap silk to give a luxurious feel, but you could choose anything from hessian to denim to velvet.

Don't forget that you'll need two finished sides for the cosy, which will be stitched together later on. We used different colours of silk – green on one side, blue on the other – but you can experiment with different types of fabric.

◀ *Tracing round the paper template on to fabric*

▶ *Machine stitching pattern through both layers of fabric*

Place the layers of fabric and wadding carefully into an embroidery ring so the fabric is left tight and unwrinkled. Set the machine to free machine embroidery (with the teeth dropped and with a free machine or darning foot). Then begin filling in the fabric with decorative stitch. This attaches the two layers together, and also gives a surface pattern. In our example, the pattern has been made up with lots of interlocking circles of different sizes which were all created using a straight stitch.

When you've finished stitching one side of the cosy, pop it out of the embroidery ring and repeat the process for the second side. You don't have to use the same pattern or type of stitch on both sides!

▶ *Finished surface stitched decoration*

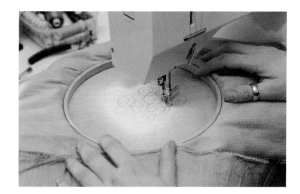

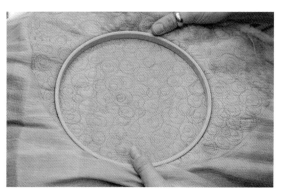

◀ *Stick reference images to a window so you can trace them*

Using masking tape or ordinary sticky tape, fix your reference sketches or designs to a window. During the day-time, the strong light from outside will act like a light box – allowing you to see the images through a thin piece of fabric.

Use more tape to secure your chosen fabric over the paper design, and then use a fine marker pen, biro or pencil to draw each image on to the fabric.

Top tip   Pick a fairly lightweight and transparent
           fabric – here, we've chosen white raw silk.

◀ *Tracing the image on to fabric*

▶ *Ironing heat-fix web on to decorative cut-outs*

Find either strongly contrasting plain fabric scraps to create appliqué shapes, or use decorative fabrics – printed or embroidered – and cut out shapes to further embellish the design. Then, iron small pieces of heat-fix web on to the back of the cut-outs and trim the shapes neatly.

With the iron set to a medium heat, iron the cut-out shapes on to the backing fabric to fix the adhesive web.

▶ *Positioning cut-out shapes on to design*

▼ *Peeling backing paper off the heat-fix web*

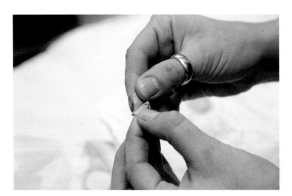

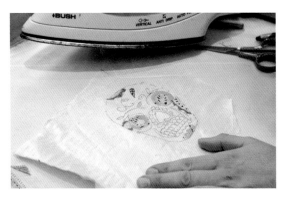

▲ *Ironing a cut-out eye on to the skull*

Top tip   If you're unsure how a material will stand up to heat, place a clean cloth over the work before ironing.

◀ *Skull with decorative shapes fixed, ready to sew*

▲ *Free machine embroidering into the design*

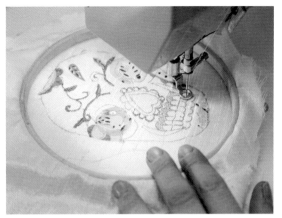

▲ *Free machine embroidery using different coloured threads*

Stretch the work tightly into an embroidery ring. Then, with the machine set as before for free machine embroidery, place the work on to the machine bed and stitch into the design. You need to stitch through the cut-out shapes, because heat-fixed web adhesive isn't really permanent; the stitching is functional as well as decorative.

Here we've used several different coloured threads and have swapped between zig-zag and straight stitches to create lots of visual variety.

Your design will stand out best when it's stitched on to the cosy if you outline it using a strong colour. Here we've used a black thread.

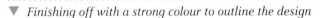

▼ *Finishing off with a strong colour to outline the design*

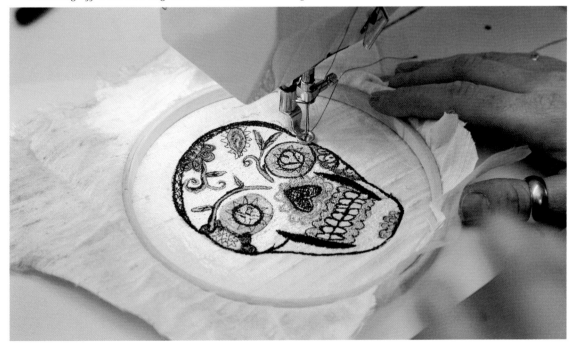

▶ *Trimming around the skull*

Using a sharp pair of small scissors, carefully trim around the design – always staying close to the sewn outline.

Using an old doily, piece of antique lace or even a big floral design from some patterned fabric, cut out shapes for the base of the flowers. These will then be appliquéd on to the cosy at a later stage (see p.108).

▶ *Cutting shapes out of doily or lace*

◀ *Cutting strips of fabric to form flower heads or buds*

Select suitable plain or printed fabric to make the flower heads or buds. Once this is done, cut long thin strips from your choice (around 3–4 cm wide).

Lay two fabric strips of the same length and width together.

Top tip   If you're using printed fabric, be sure to lay the two plain faces together with the printed designs facing outwards.

◀ *Laying fabric strips together before stitching*

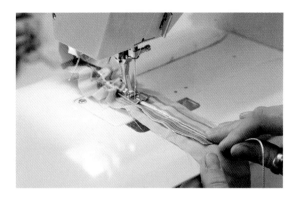

Raise the teeth on your sewing machine and also add a normal straight stitch or zig-zag stitch foot. Starting at one end of the fabric strips, lay the elastic thread down the middle of the top strip. Zig-zag forwards and backwards to hold the end of the elastic tightly in place, and then pull the thread tightly with one hand to create tension while you zig-zag stitch down the middle. This attaches the elastic to the fabric strips while gathering them at the same time – a technique called 'ruching'.

To create the illusion of frilly petals like those found on a carnation, snip carefully into the edges of the fabric strips. Be careful not to cut through the elastic! The closer your snips are together, the more frills your flower will have.

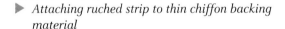

▶ *Cutting into the edges of the ruched fabric*

▶ *Attaching ruched strip to thin chiffon backing material*

Place a piece of very thin net, silk or chiffon in the embroidery ring. With the machine set to a small zig-zag stitch and the teeth dropped (as for free machine embroidery), hold one end of the ruched strip in the middle of the ring, and then zig-zag over to secure it to the backing fabric.

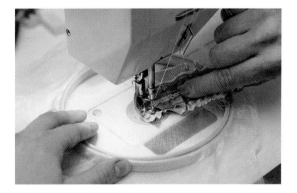

As you zig-zag, slowly turn the material around the needle so as to form a tightly stitched coil of fabric. With the frayed edge on the outside of the circle, work in a clockwise direction, moving the fabric so it touches the previously stitched strip. Remember to reverse backwards and then forwards to tie off the stitch securely.

▶ *Turning the strip to form a 3-D flower effect*

▶ *A finished flower head*

Repeat this process for as many flower heads as you need. To create smaller flowers, just cut thinner strips – bigger, fatter blooms can be created using wider and longer strips. Experiment with different weights of fabric for different results, as well.

Keep the finished flower head in the ring so it's easy to manipulate and position, and then lay it over the lace cut-out 'leaves'. We've used an almost transparent chiffon which effectively disappears, letting the lacework show through. Feel free to experiment – an opaque fabric backing could also look good, for example.

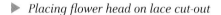

▶ *Placing flower head on lace cut-out*

◀ *Sewing around the flower to attach it to the lace base*

Hold the flower head with one hand to expose the base of the flower, and then stitch around the base – through the chiffon backing – to attach the flower and chiffon to the cut-out doily. Use a small zig-zag stitch to stop the fabric from fraying.

Carefully cut away the excess chiffon close to the base of the flower and the doily.

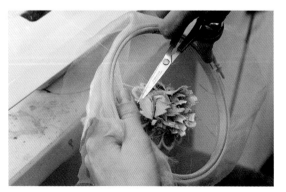

◀ *Trimming away chiffon close to the stitch line*

▶ *Gluing the edges of the flower*

Top tip   A few drops of glue on the edges of the flower petals will prevent them from fraying and keep them stiff.

Arrange the finished flowers and your main motif on the cosy.

Once you've worked out the right positions for the main elements of your design, add extra decorative details. Here we've added hearts cut out of red velvet.

▶ *Arranging flowers and motif on the background material*

▼ *Adding appliqué hearts*

All the flat appliqué elements of the design need to have heat-set adhesive web ironed on to the reverse side. When the ironing is done, peel the backing off as before and iron on to the background fabric of the cosy.

Now you can fill in even more detail by drawing freehand patterns – scrolls, arabesques or whatever else you fancy.

▲ *Drawing freehand designs to be stitched*

With the machine set for free machine embroidery (teeth dropped, darning foot attached), set a medium zig-zag stitch and satin stitch around the shapes to fix them permanently to the backing fabric. The scroll patterns here are done with the same stitch, using dark threads for contrast.

Use fabric or craft glue to fix the bottom of the flower bases to the backing fabric.

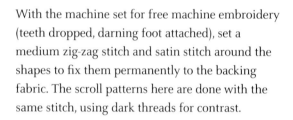

Top tip   Allow flower bases to dry before stitching so you don't get glue on your sewing machine!

▲ *Free machine embroidering and stitching over the appliqué shapes*

▲ *Gluing the bottom of the flower bases*

▶ *Sewing flower bases to background material*

Use straight or zig-zag stitching to attach the flower bases to the fabric of the cosy. Here we've used a white thread so the stitching is invisible.

To make a fabric-covered piping for inserting into the seams of the cosy, fold a piece of fabric corner to corner (to produce a triangle shape), and then cut a strip running parallel to the fold. This creates a bias binding strip (so-called because you're cutting the material on the bias, which allows it to stretch).

▶ *Folding fabric in half and cutting to produce a bias strip*

◀ *Placing piping cord in centre of bias strip*

Open out the cut bias strip and place a piece of piping cord in the middle, down the fold line (dressing gown cord or thick string is also suitable). Leave the cord or string sticking out slightly at one end.

Change the machine foot to a zipper foot and move the needle to either the left or right of the foot. Then raise the teeth. Next, stitch closely along the edge of the piping cord – remembering to reverse at the start and finish to secure the stitches.

◀ *Enclosing cord in bias binding*

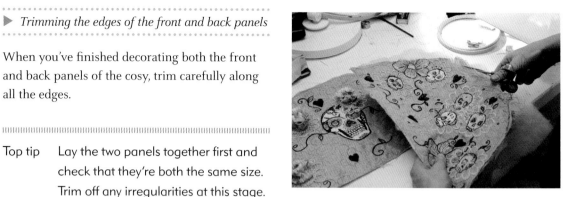

▶ *Trimming the edges of the front and back panels*

When you've finished decorating both the front and back panels of the cosy, trim carefully along all the edges.

Top tip   Lay the two panels together first and check that they're both the same size. Trim off any irregularities at this stage.

Pin the piped binding to the edge of one side of the cosy, with the piped edge as the inside (towards the design) and the 'raw' edge facing outwards. When you come to stitch both sides together, the raw edge will be on the outside of the cosy.

▲ *Pinning piped binding to edge seam of one side of cosy*

◀ *Stitching around the outside of the piped binding*

Still with the zipper foot on, move the needle to the left and sew closely along the edge of the piping cord.

With the two 'right' sides of the cosy panels together, place a loop of thin piping cord or bias binding at the top of the semi-circle with the cut ends facing outwards.

◀ *Positioning lifting loop on top of cosy*

▶ *Pinning the two panels together*

Pin along the outer seam – as closely to the piped binding as is possible.

Still using the zipper foot, sew along the outside of the piped binding.

Using the same paper or card template that you made for the two main panels of the cosy, subtract 2 cm or so from the width and height, and then trace and cut two lining panels from any suitable fabric. Pin these two panels together.

Change the foot to a normal straight stitch or zig-zag foot, and with the teeth up, stitch the two lining panels together along the semi-circle with a small (1 cm) seam allowance.

▶ *Sewing the two panels together*

▼ *Turning the cosy through*

▲ *Sewing a liner*

Turn the open (bottom) edges of the liner upwards like a trouser turn-up, and iron to make a crease.

◀ *Ironing turned edges of liner*

113

Carefully insert the liner into the cosy until the creased edges are flush with the cosy's bottom.

▲ *Inserting the liner into the cosy*

If you plan to leave the bottom of your cosy plain, turn the top panel under, and then press it into position with the iron. Next, pin the edges of the top panel and the liner together before sewing.

▲ *Stitching along the bottom edges of the cosy*

Here we've decided to use a feather trim along the bottom of the cosy, so we've zig-zag stitched the two layers together – the feather trim will hide the raw edge.

Using a zig-zag stitch, sew through the feather trim and along the bottom seam of the cosy.

▲ *Sewing feather trim to the bottom of the cosy*

El cosy completado y el hombre muerto!

Glossary

▲ *Superglue and other adhesives are useful for fixing parts of your work.*

▲ *Heat-fixed web adhesive is ironed on to the back of fabric to be attached, then the paper backing is peeled off and the web-backed fabric is ironed on to the work below.*

ADHESIVES IIIIIIIIIIIIIIIIIIIIIIIIIIIIIIIIIIIIIIIIIIII

Adhesives can be used in textile work as an alternative to stitching. PVA adhesive is also used to make papier maché.

Special heat-fixed web adhesive (or 'Bondaweb') is quick and easy to use for sticking flat surfaces together, e.g. bonding one layer of fabric to another. It irons on, doesn't leave a sticky residue and leaves a smooth wrinkle-free surface.

APPLIQUÉ IIIIIIIIIIIIIIIIIIIIIIIIIIIIIIIIIIIIIIIIIIIIII

A French word that basically means attaching one piece of fabric on top of another. Can be done by hand sewing, machine stitching or gluing.

▲ *Appliqué details are anything that can be applied to flat surfaces. Here felt hearts, lace flowers and a stitched skull are being attached to background fabric.*

An appliqué design is usually cut out and then attached a background. This technique has a huge number of variations giving different decorative effects.

ARMATURE ||||||||||||||||||||||||||||||||||||||

A term borrowed from sculpture that refers to the basic framework or skeleton of a modelled object. An armature needs to be fairly rigid, so wire is commonly used. But wood, pipework and rigid containers such as plastic bottles can all be used. See also WIREFRAME.

'BOIL-AWAY' FABRIC |||||||||||||||||||||||||||

see WATER SOLUBLE FABRIC

BURNING ||||||||||||||||||||||||||||||||||||||||

A pyrographic tool is a useful addition to the textile artist's toolkit. Its interchangeable, electrically-heated tips allow you to burn different patterns and effects into materials such as leather (shown here), plastics, foam, thick card, man-made fabrics and even thin slices of wood.

CASTING ||||||||||||||||||||||||||||||||||||||||

This involves a liquid material such as metal, clay, cement or liquid latex (shown here) which is poured, painted or sprayed into a pre-formed mould. The most useful application of this technique in textile art is to make thin, flexible rubber objects that can be stuck or sewn on to work.

An interesting variation once you have made a mould is to press thin rolled paperclay or fibrous clay into the mould and then fire it – remembering to leave holes in the objects so you can sew them on. Or you can make a soft flour dough, press it into the mould and then bake the cast shapes into tiny bread decorations to sew into your work.

▲ *This wire armature forms the frame or skeleton of a bird*

▲ *Using a pyrographic tool to burn patterns into leather*

▲ *Casting latex shapes in a plaster mould*

CUTWORK ||||||||||||||||||||||||||||||||||||||||||||||

Cutwork is usually achieved by stitching together layers of fabric of different weights and colours, and then cutting away one or more layers to reveal the contrasting colours, textures and patterns beneath.

Always take care to stitch outlines around the shapes to be cut away – this prevents fraying.

EMBROIDERY RING ||||||||||||||||||||||||||||||||||||

Holds the work taut to allow easier free-machining or hand sewing. Rings can be made of wood, plastic and metal.

For free machining, put the ring with the adjustable screw on the bottom, then the fabric and then the other half of the ring, and pull the fabric tight as if a drumskin.

For hand sewing, have the adjustable screw on top.

When using a ring with very fine work, or where the ring will mark the fabric (such as with the pile on a velvet), the ring can be bound with fabric to prevent this.

FABRICS ||||||||||||||||||||||||||||||||||||||||||||||||

Woven fabrics split into two types: natural (cotton, silk, calico, linen, wool, hessian) and man-made or synthetic (polyesters, rayons, acetates, viscose, acrylics). There are also many fibre mixes – poly/cotton is the most common, and mixes which incorporate stretch materials such as Lycra and jersey. And there are non-woven fabrics such as felt and leather, plus laminated fabrics.

Certain fabrics can be either natural or man-made – silks, velvets, laces and chiffons, for example. Surface textures can be decorative (for example printing, stencilling, flocking, devoré, moiré, embossing) or functional (cording, waterproofing, fire retardant etc.)

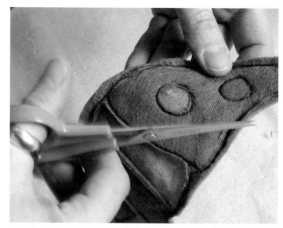

▲ *Cutwork exposes different layers of fabric to give extra depth*

▲ *Holding fabric tightly in an embroidery ring allows easier stitching*

▲ *Fabrics come in many weights, finishes and textures*

It's a great idea to pick up fabric scraps whenever you see them – bits of worn-out clothes, leftovers from upholstery- or curtain-making, interesting packaging etc.

▲ *Fabric pens, crayons and markers*

Top tip   Keep fabrics sorted in bags according to purpose and type – for example, leathers and furs together; denims and canvas together, silks with chiffons etc.

FABRIC PENS, CRAYONS & MARKERS

Special pens and markers for drawing, outlining and adding detail on fabrics. Sometimes sold as 'T-shirt markers'; different types are available for use on other fabrics. Some markers can be heat-fixed to give permanent results (see IRONING OFF).

FOUND OBJECTS

Natural or man-made items that can be added to work as decoration (for example: shells, broken pottery). Also objects that can be used as templates for shapes, patterns and moulds (for example: glasses, cutlery, kitchen utensils).

Some found objects also make great printing blocks or stencils.

▲ *Found objects can be used as models for latex casting.*

FRINGING

Decorative edging effect produced by cutting or slashing the outer edge of a piece of fabric.

GATHERING

This technique uses the tension of elastic to pull fabric together into ruffles by making a shorter length. It is useful for decorative work such as making flower centres and creating fancy edgings.

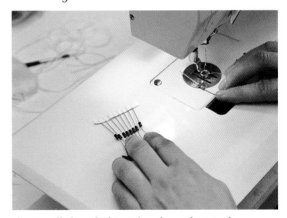

▲ *Small 'found objects' such as electrical components, broken jewellery, plastic toys and jigsaw pieces can be sewn into textile work.*

▲ *Fringing the edges of flower petals*

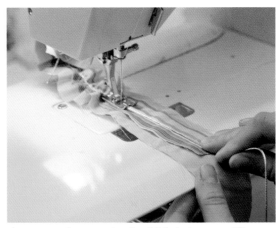

▲ *Using elastic to 'gather' fabric into a ruffle*

IRONING OFF ||||||||||||||||||||||||||||||||||||||

Ironing off is used to fix web adhesive or fabric paint by means of heat. Cover the work with a clean cloth. With the iron set on 'high', hold in place for a couple of seconds.

If you are using fabric paint, the top cloth absorbs excess paint as well as protecting the work.

MOULD MAKING ||||||||||||||||||||||||||||||||||||

This goes hand-in-hand with CASTING. Ordinary pottery clay is used to make a casing into which you can set found objects (shown here) to cast copies. Or you can simply form a shallow relief shape such as a leaf on the clay slab. Whichever method you choose, you then pour plaster mixture over the objects to be moulded. Once the plaster has dried and the clay is removed, you have a reusable mould.

NEEDLES ||||||||||||||||||||||||||||||||||||||||||||

Needles come in different thicknesses and lengths depending on purpose.

MACHINE NEEDLES vary slightly in design according to machine type. Always select a machine needle of the correct size and point for the fabric

▲ *Ironing off with a clean cloth over the work*

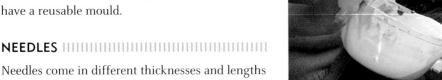

▲ *Pouring plaster to make a reusable mould*

and thread you choose. The smaller the number on the needle, the finer it is: size 70 is a very fine needle used for lightweight fabrics. Bigger numbers denote coarser needles for heavier fabrics.

The needle is held in place by the needle clamp. This can be loosened off with the clamp screw to remove a needle, and then tightened up after a new needle has been inserted into the clamp.

HAND SEWING NEEDLES come in a wide range of lengths and thicknesses. For general hand sewing, these are usually 'sharps', which are medium length and suitable for almost all fabric weights. Embroidery needles tend to have a larger eye. Tapestry needles are thicker and blunter, with a big eye suitable for wools and thick threads.

PAINTS ||||||||||||||||||||||||||||||||||||||||||||||||

ACRYLIC A water-based plastic paint that is thick and gives strong, solid colours. It is not ideal for use on fabric as it sits on the surface and tends to flake off if fabric is folded or sewn into. But acrylic is ideal for painting wood, paper, card etc. It can also be used to colour liquid latex when making casts.

FABRIC PAINT Most fabric paints are water-based. They are wash-resistant after they have been fixed using heat (see IRONING OFF). Gloss, 'bright', glitter, pearl and metallic paints are available, and these can be mixed to give a wide variety of effects. Fabric paint sticks are also available – these are more like wax crayons to use.

PAPIER MACHÉ ||||||||||||||||||||||||||||||||||||||||

Torn paper/glue mixture that can be built up in layers to create a durable form. Classic papier maché is newsprint and wallpaper paste, mulched up and applied in layers. Variants include: using PVA instead of wallpaper paste; screwing up

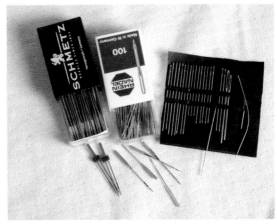

▲ *A selection of machine needles (left) and hand sewing needles (right)*

▲ *Acrylic paint gives solid colours. It is good for painting papier maché, wood and card*

▲ *A selection of fabric paints*

▲ *Building up papier maché on a wire armature to form a body*

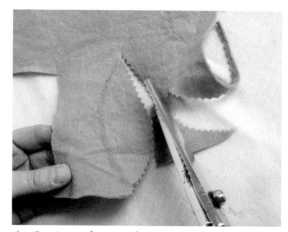

▲ *Cutting a shape with zigzag 'pinked' edges using pinking shears*

dried newspaper and then using masking tape to create the form, then adding the mulch; or using strips of newspaper dipped in PVA glue and smoothed over a form.

PINKING ||||||||||||||||||||||||||||||||||||||||||||||

Is the name given to the tooth-like zigzag edge produced by special scissors called pinking shears. Pinking is both decorative and functional – the pinked edges prevent the work from fraying.

PIPING |||||||||||||||||||||||||||||||||||||||||||||||||

Refers to a special type of twisted cord ('piping cord') or any other cord-like object (wire, string, thick wool) which is wrapped in fabric. The fabric is usually cut 'on the bias' to give stretch. A bias is created by folding a strip of fabric diagonally (corner to corner), then cut parallel to the fold.

When the cord has been encased, sew along the edge of the cord using a zipper foot.

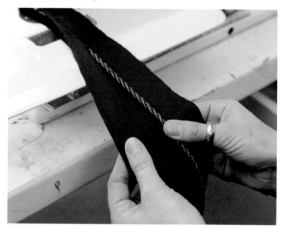

▲ *Creating a piping strip by wrapping a piping cord in fabric*

PRIMER/PRIMING |||||||||||||||||||||||||||||||||||||||

A base coat of paint to seal the surface of papier maché, wood, fabric etc.

▲ *A thick coat of emulsion or acrylic can be used to prime a surface*

PYROGRAPHY ||||||||||||||||||||||||||||||||||||

The proper name for BURNING a design into material such leather, plastic or wood. It's best to use a special electric pyrographic tool with a selection of tips.

SEAM ALLOWANCE ||||||||||||||||||||||||||||||

The border or margin left outside the stitch line. The seam allowance can be functional: it provides an edge for sewing two pieces of fabric together; and it can also prevent fraying. It can also be a decorative feature. A small seam allowance is also used so that decorative or reinforcing edging can be added.

STITCHES ||||||||||||||||||||||||||||||||||||||||||||

MACHINE EMBROIDERY The term for any stitch produced by a sewing machine. The most commonly used stitches are 'running' and 'zig-zag' stitches, which are basic dressmaking stitches. These use the presser foot and have the teeth up, enabling the fabric to be guided through the machine. The weight of the presser foot can be adjusted depending on the weight of the fabric.

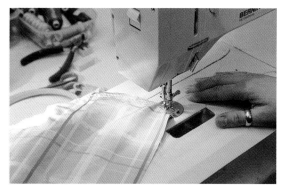

▲ *Here we've used a 1cm seam allowance around the edges of this cosy liner*

These simple machine stitches are used for outlining, attaching and seaming. A short stitch length makes it easier to manoeuvre the presser foot around curves.

Pre-set or programmed stitch patterns are available on most sewing machines.

FREE MACHINE EMBROIDERY is a more creative technique that allows the user to 'draw' with the thread. The machine's teeth or feed must be able to be dropped into the bed or covered, so the fabric is not gripped. This can be done by

▲ *Free machine embroidery foot (or darning foot) with the teeth down*

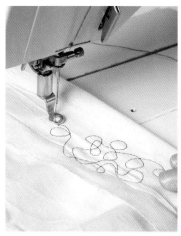

▲ *Free machine embroidery using a straight stitch*

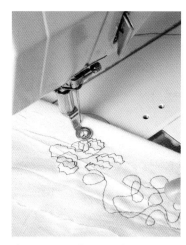

▲ *Free machine embroidery using a zig-zag stitch*

lifting a lever to lower the teeth or using a cover plate. Instead of the teeth gripping the fabric, you are in complete control of the direction in which you stitch. You can move the work up, down, sideways and around the needle – or in any combination. It's a bit like drawing with a pencil.

It is easier to free machine embroider if work is placed in an EMBROIDERY RING. This sits on the bed of the machine and can be moved around the needle freely.

For the projects in this book, we have used a free machine embroidery foot. The foot is an important safety feature that shields the needle: do not remove it when working with children!

Some experienced textile artists prefer to free machine embroider without using a foot. This is only possible if the fabric is stretched really tight, and if the work is not too layered, thick or bulky.

HAND STITCHING Hand stitching can be functional or decorative. In its functional role, it is used for attaching fasteners such as zips, buttons or Velcro; or for joining two seams; or for attaching components together.

In its decorative role, hand stitch can be used to work in thick threads or even wire. And it's essential to attach beads, sequins, found objects such as shells, twigs or pierced pottery fragments.

STUFFING ||||||||||||||||||||||||||||||||||||||||||||||

Any technique that involves filling two stitched panels with material such as wadding, cotton wool, polystyrene foam or chips to create a three-dimensional effect.

It's best to stitch round the area to be stuffed, with a backing fabric behind, to create a closed pocket. Then cut a slit in the backing, stuff the filler in, then sew up the slit.

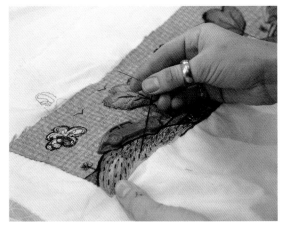

▲ *Decorative hand stitching*

▲ *Stuffing wadding through a slit in the back of work*

▲ *Card templates for flower shapes*

124

TEMPLATE ||||||||||||||||||||||||||||||||||||||||

A shape or pattern made of card, plastic sheet or cloth which is used to make duplicate shapes.

THREADS ||||||||||||||||||||||||||||||||||||||||

Threads come in almost as many varieties as fabrics. They are made of different types of yarn (polyesters, cottons, wools, silks, mixes) and are available in a huge range of colours.

Hand sewing threads tend to be thicker, with more strands than machine thread. Some can even have metallic strands twisted into them. Hand sewing threads usually come loosely wound on reels or in skeins or hanks.

Most machine threads come tightly wound on a spool or bobbin – this ensures that the tension remains constant when the yarn is threaded on to a sewing machine. They come in different weights – a 30 is suitable for heavier fabrics, a 60 is lighter.

Always try to choose the right thread for the purpose – a heavy fabric will tend to need a heavier thread, while silks and chiffons need a very lightweight one.

TRAPUNTO QUILTING |||||||||||||||||||||||||||

A specialist technique borrowed from quilting for stuffing a three-dimensional textile object. Essentially the same as STUFFING.

TRIMMING ||||||||||||||||||||||||||||||||||||||

Cutting around shapes to remove excess fabric and leave a neat edge. Use small sharp scissors but be careful not to cut through stitches!

TYING OFF ||||||||||||||||||||||||||||||||||||||

Prevents stitches coming undone.
To tie off by hand, make a knot or several small

▲ *A selection of hand sewing threads (above) and machine threads (below)* ▼

▲ *Trimming away excess material around an appliqué design*

stitches in the same place, then cut the thread (but not too close to the knot!)

By machine, go forwards and backwards over the same part of the work – this is called over-sewing.

WATER SOLUBLE FABRIC ||||||||||||||||||||||||||||

A specialist fabric that can be stitched decoratively with threads and wires, then dissolved away using either hot or cold water. Hot water soluble fabric is sometimes called 'boil-away' because it can be dissolved in a kettle or pan of boiling water.

▲ *Water soluble fabric can be 'boiled away'*

WIREFRAME ||||||||||||||||||||||||||||||||||||||||||||

Stitching wire around an outline shape gives rigidity that allows a two-dimensional piece of fabric to be manipulated into a three-dimensional form – e.g. the wings of a bird or petals of a flower.

▲ *Stitching a wireframe into fabric to give rigidity*

Index